five +one

The Entrepreneurs
Formula for Success

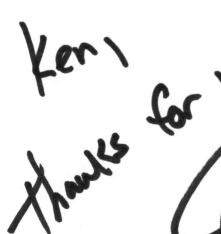

Ken,
Thanks for your support!

Chas Wilson

Five + One =
The Entrepreneurs Formula for Success

Published by Master Networks Publishing
www.MasterNetworksPublishing.com

ISBN: 978-1-943157-04-4

Printed in the United States of America

For more information or to reach the author, go to:

www.FiveplusOneBook.com

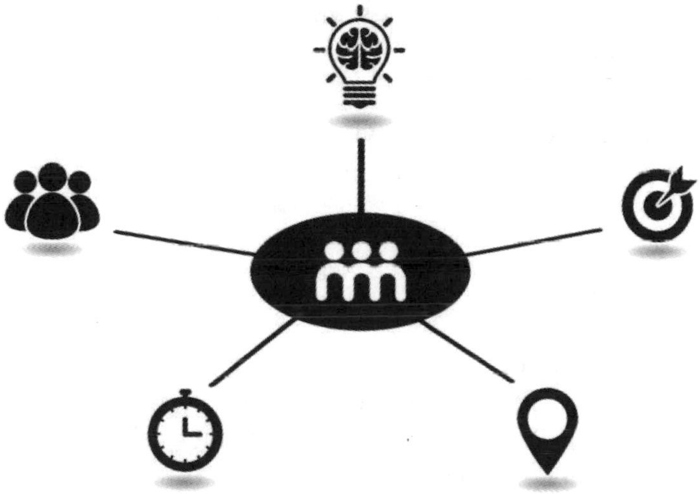

DEDICATION

Like you, I am an entrepreneur at heart. And like you, it is in me to keep pressing forward until I find the answers that take business to the next level! I'm always pressing forward. I can't help it. And neither can you!

For me, my date with destiny was January 2, 2011. It is a date I will forever remember!

My business partner and I met at a Panera Bread Restaurant to discuss and mastermind some of our ideas over lunch. Like many times before, we made a list of different ways we could start a business that would have a large impact, serve many, and be highly profitable.

I wrote several ideas down, and pretty quickly we had developed a concept for our company. I had made similar lists before, but this time was different. I vividly remember looking at the sheet of paper with our notes and bullet points, thinking to myself, "We have to *do* something this time. We *have* to do this!"

So we got started. We didn't have it all figured out, but we just took the first few steps forward. Three months later, we officially launched Master Networks, Inc.

Every day since then, I have been blessed to associate with a special group of people just like you: entrepreneurs. They are a unique group who drive their local economies, employ others, and support communities.

In this book, I want to invite you on a journey of discovery to find the keys that unlock the mystery and power of business success. Let's get after it!

TABLE OF CONTENTS

INTRODUCTION

Entrepreneurs and business leaders are not typically understood by those around them. The government definitely doesn't understand the local business owner. Friends and family do their best to support them but have a hard time knowing what they really do.

As entrepreneurs and business leaders, we have the great opportunity and responsibility to help support our local communities and revitalize the economy. Together we can!

The Challenge

More than ever, people are stepping into the world of entrepreneurship. That is the good news! The bad news is that many of these people are entering the world of entrepreneurship with little to no understanding of how to be successful.

> Why do 8 out of 10 businesses fail within the first 18 months?

I have read recently that as many as 8 out of 10 businesses will fail within the first 18 months. That is an incredible 80% failure rate! At first glance, most people would say that is because of the lack of money. True, the lack of money often shows up as the result that leads to the failure of the business, but believe me, the cracks in the foundation happened long before the money ran low.

So why is there such a failure rate and what can you do to protect yourself from these seemingly insurmountable odds?

You have heard the phrase, "When the student is ready, the teacher appears." I believe when the student is ready, the student seeks out the teacher!

Reading books like this and surrounding yourself with successful mentors will support you in taking your first step.

The Eight Truths of an Entrepreneur

I am fascinated with the strength, character, and focus of the entrepreneur. As I have studied, researched, and developed my own skills as an entrepreneur, I discovered eight truths.

> *Entrepreneurs must work ON their business every week, month, and year.* They understand how important it is to set time in their hectic and demanding lives to work ON their business, not just IN their business. They find a quiet place to think, explore, and envision the future of their company, position, role, or opportunity.

> *Entrepreneurs are willing to do what is uncomfortable.* This is courage in its truest form. Who naturally and easily wants to make cold calls, to speak in public, and to do what they don't necessarily have the skills to do? Few would ever sign up for that, but entrepreneurs do it every day! They do what is uncomfortable because they want the end result – to achieve their goals. Along the way, they become better (skills improve) and their confidence grows.

> *Entrepreneurs overcome fears on purpose.* They have fears like everyone else, but they address those fears head on. They believe they can handle them, and they do, which further adds to their self-confidence. If they are afraid of something (i.e. speaking from stage), they care more about

the desired outcome (i.e. delivering a message), so they do it anyway! In time, they know they will win.

Entrepreneurs encourage themselves. They use positive self-talk and pep talks on themselves. Why? Because the mind can easily generate negative thoughts that lead down the trail toward anxiety, worry, and even depression. These thoughts can undermine success. The positive self-talk encourages them to keep going and believe. Sometimes, those words are the difference between achieving the impossible and not even coming close.

Entrepreneurs overcome limiting beliefs. We all have limiting thoughts or ideas from our past that need to be fixed. If we don't, those thoughts can hurt us. It's the proverbial "skeletons in the closet" or "baggage," but either way, entrepreneurs don't settle for that's-just-the-way-it-is thinking. No! They deal with things and work on overcoming limiting beliefs. They break it down and beat it into the ground!

Entrepreneurs choose encouraging relationships. They are careful about the friends they choose. They purposefully gather positive people around them and actively avoid negative people if at all possible. Obviously, family members can't be avoided, but the choice to allow the negativity to sink in or just let it bounce off is always up to them!

Entrepreneurs celebrate all the challenges met and the progress made along the way. The journey is important, and entrepreneurs know how to celebrate the small victories: obstacles overcome, challenges met, steps taken. It's all worth celebrating.

Entrepreneurs encourage and inspire others. Entrepreneurs are positive role models; that is for sure. They provide this gift to every staff member, their family, their local community, and, in the ultimate sense, their nation and the world.

The Five Disciplines and the One Master Skill

Over the past 15 years in business, I have made many mistakes and learned many hard lessons. But I have done many things right. What I have come to understand is that there is a simple path and track to follow that will help you be successful in any business.

I have spent the last few years traveling the country, teaching what you will learn in this book. The feedback I have received has been instructional and inspirational. Many of the attendees, my customers, and consulting clients have been instrumental in driving me to write this book.

> There is a simple path and track to follow that will help you be successful in any business.

Read this book all the way through. Take notes. Go back through it section by section and make an action plan to implement that speaks to you.

My hope for you is that you can build a business that is at a level of success you define, allows you the money to have the freedom you desire, and serves your life in a way that allows you to live your purpose.

CHAPTER ONE

THINKING

*The attitude you take into a venture
will impact how it turns out.*

*Build the correct mindset
before you dive in!*

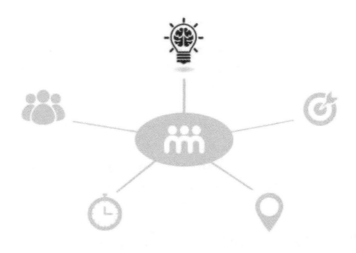

THINKING: PART #1

—THE FIRST DISCIPLINE: THINKING

As business owners and leaders, we are the creative designers of our ventures. We are the architects of our future. We do this most effectively by mastering the first discipline of business: THINKING.

We understand that nothing good happens by accident and that we must make it happen with our own visioning, planning, and goal setting. This is how we:

- create the reality we intend
- make things happen
- get what we want

It takes years to truly master the skill of THINKING. It is a complex and demanding process. It is often the truest measure of our maturity as a business leader.

On a regular weekly, monthly, and yearly basis, we find a quiet place where we can think, where we can explore, where we can look for new options and better ways. By taking the time to imagine, invent and plan, we find ways to improve, enhance, and expand.

 We then take action more effectively, get more things done and achieve more results. The better we get at missioning, visioning, and planning, the more control we have and the more influence we exert. We become the architects of our businesses and of our own personal destiny.

Mindset

Mindset is the way you think and how you think, but it is not necessarily what you are thinking. Some call it a set of beliefs about how things work and how we look at the world.

The mindset of an entrepreneur begins with a deep respect for freedom, enterprise and opportunity. World history is full of tyranny and slavery and coercing others through brute force and oppression. Life, liberty, and the pursuit of happiness are deeply rooted values for the entrepreneurs.

> Entrepreneurs believe in abundance.

They understand that there are no guarantees, but the right to choose is what fuels their belief in the power of freedom.

Entrepreneurs believe in abundance. They know that there is more than enough for everyone and plenty of everything to go around. But they are also fiercely competitive. They know that they must earn their share of the abundance. They understand that it comes as a result of hard work and effort. They take personal responsibility and are accountable for their own results.

High Achiever vs. Entrepreneur

High Achievers are the work horses. They understand that to get what they want they need to take action. High Achievers adopt the cry:

If it's to be, it's up to me.

Entrepreneurs typically start as High Achievers and quickly find themselves saying, "There must be a better way." They move to adopt systems and models to leverage and maximize their efforts.

Consider the table below:

High Achiever	Entrepreneur
Says, "What needs to be done and how can I do it?"	Says, "What needs to be done and who can I get to do it?"
Works Harder to achieve results	Works Smarter to maximize results
Works for others	Works through others
Seizes Opportunities	Creates Opportunities
Hits Ceiling of Achievement	Implements models and systems to break through the ceilings

THINKING: PART #2

—CRAFTING A VISION & MISSION STATEMENT

Some entrepreneurs end up changing the world. Henry Ford, Thomas Edison, Sam Walton, and Steve Jobs are among the many who have. But most business owners and leaders do their visionary work on a more pragmatic and local level. They create ventures, products, and services that weren't there before. They provide jobs and opportunities and investments. They create assets and value.

More than anything, they believe in and create things that others just dream about. Entrepreneurs are dreamers, but they are also doers. They take action and make things happen.

Therefore, we don't call them "dreamers" (the world has enough of those), we call them "visionaries." They see, they plan, they act, and they create – and that is a far cry from just dreaming!

But before anything gets created, there is a dream or vision for what is possible and the path to make it so.

You may have heard the great proverb, "Where there is no vision, the people will perish." The opposite is also true. Where there is vision, the people will flourish!

Take time to dream about your business, your enterprise, and your venture. What will it look like? Who will be in it? Who will be served and how?

Where will it be located? What will be happening? What will it do for you, your family, friends, and community? What do you see for the future? Remember, what you see is what you will get. In fact, it is what you will create!

Entrepreneurs and business leaders are visionaries. Not that they can predict the future, but they can see what is possible and make it happen. In truth, they create the future.

Crafting your vision statement

Vision statements set a high level, big picture of the future that your organization hopes to attain. Most organizations are not yet living their vision because it is something they are working toward.

Your vision statement notes the purpose of your organization and states the values and beliefs that your organization works under. Here are some questions to ponder as you begin to craft your vision statement:

- What do you envision your company to be in the future?

- What size do you want your company to be? (Will it be small with a few employees or large with a regional, national, or global reach with a lot of employees?)

As an example, here is the vision statement of Master Networks:

 Master Networks is the fastest growing, most innovative and rewarding networking organization in North America. Master Networks will have at least 5,000 chapters and 125,000 members in North America.

Take your time. Craft a vision statement that best defines who you are, what you do, and where you are going. And as you take strides forward, feel free to tweak your vision and statement as needed.

It's not set in stone. That would be your epitaph, which is an entirely different sort of mission and vision statement. But let your vision statement evolve over time.

> Before anything gets created, there is a dream or vision for what is possible and the path to make it so.

Committing time and energy to create and document a mission statement and a vision statement is very powerful. These statements tell you, and everyone around you, just what you are doing and where you are heading.

Here are a few reasons to take the time to craft your vision:

- ✓ The exercise of creating the statements forces you to clearly identify your current focus and the focus of your organization.

- ✓ You and your organization can gain a clear picture of where you would like to go next.

- ✓ The two statements will be a message to employees on the purpose and direction of your organization.

- ✓ The words on paper, when translated into actions and behaviors, can build or change the world!

Your mission statement

A mission statement is designed to explain precisely

what your organization does. It spells out the purpose and primary objective of your company's existence.

One immediate benefit is that once this is in place, employees can then take their role and duties and relate at a higher level with the purpose of the organization. Similarly, customers can see that the meeting of their needs is a purposeful part of your existence, and they will love you and refer others to you as a result!

Here are questions to answer during the development of your mission statement:

- What do we do?
- Why do we exist?
- What products and/or services do we offer?
- What problem do we solve?
- What need or desire do we meet?
- How do we create value?
- Who finds value in our products and/or services
- Whom do we serve?

Here is an example of Master Networks Mission Statement:

> We are a membership network of learning-based, service-oriented entrepreneurs and business leaders. We meet in local chapters, powered by national and regional platforms, to connect, share, and prosper.

Words Matter

Entrepreneurs learn to be really good with words. Not like a writer or journalist, but more like an evangelist and promoter. At the end of the day, entrepreneurs understand that they are the leaders and the motivators. They have the vision, they know their value proposition, and they need to teach others about their ventures.

No one else can really write it for you, though others can help clean it up. The power of these statements comes from how much you believe what is written. That's why it needs to come from you.

There is magic in the words you use, so experiment with them, master them, and communicate them to the world.

THINKING: PART #3

—CREATING S.M.A.R.T. GOALS

In business, if you don't have your own plan, you'll be part of somebody else's.

S.M.A.R.T. GOALS

Clear, focused targets are much more powerful than abstract and hazy ones. There is a formula for creating great goals: it's called the **SMART** method. S-M-A-R-T is an acronym, which stands for the five words that should be true for goals that empower actions and achieve desired results.

S is for Specific: Goals that are specific use precise numbers and details. They should not be general or vague. "I want to make more money" is way too general to be a motivating goal. "I want to increase profits from $100,000 to $200,000 by the end of the year" is very specific. So is the goal: "To increase our customer satisfaction rates to 8.5 out of 10."

M is for Measurable: Your goal should have an outcome that can be tracked, counted, and known. You will know then when it is achieved. It has been long said:

If you can measure it, then you can manage it.

 The exact opposite is usually the case in people's personal lives and in their businesses:

If you can't measure it, you can't manage it.

Obviously, you want to be able to measure it, and when your goals are measurable, then anyone can see you have achieved it by simply looking at the results. The proof is in the numbers! Whatever it is you want to accomplish or do, you must be able to track it.

A *is for Action-oriented:* Goals should have action words that indicate what will be done. It needs to be inspiring. Words like *cause, sell, increase, grow, achieve, impact,* or *empower* are helpful in defining your goal.

> Goal setting is a process, not an event.

The bottom line is that the words will empower YOU to take action. It is, after all, your goal. You want you to take determined action. So craft your goal in such a way that you can't help but be motivated to get after it.

R *is for Realistic:* This is not a negative word or a way to minimize a goal. Rather, it helps clarify the goal and make it more powerful. A truly realistic goal will stretch and challenge. It may have a 50/50 chance of being accomplished.

If the goal is impossible, such as "I'm going to make $1 million next year," and all you've ever made is $50,000 working in an industry or job that cannot get you more than a 3% increase, then truly that goal is NOT realistic. To set a goal that stretches you to make $60,000 would be realistic and motivating.

Remember, goals should inspire you, push you, and move you closer and closer to your highest potential.

T *is for Time bound:* Goals must have a timeline or deadline for their accomplishment. It should create a sense of urgency. It's a deadline after all!

The due date should push you forward. It makes you want to get up and get it done. Whether the deadline is the end of the week, month, year, or decade, it should propel you forward.

Do it right, shine the light

The goals and plans of your business become even more powerful when they are shared. Many business owners make the mistake of playing it close to the vest. They keep their employees in the dark. They seek no input or advice from others. This is a mistake that can stunt both growth and profitability.

Sam Walton, in his book *Made in America,* outlines "the ten rules that worked for me." He said, "...treat your associates as partners..." and "...communicate everything you possibly can. The more they know, the more they'll understand. The more they understand, the more they'll care. Once they care, there's no stopping them. Information is power."

> Goals should inspire you, push you, and move you closer to your highest potential.

Let everyone know your vision for the business, which includes your goals, plans, and intentions. Tell your leaders, employees, friends, and even your customers. Then they will get excited and energized. They will bring ideas, potential new employees, and prospective customers. They will sense what is needed and make it so.

Better yet, involve them in the planning process. Have a planning meeting or retreat. Ask them provocative questions, like "What if we could..." or "How would we..." or "What improvements are possible?" It's not just open-ended and it's not a pure democracy. You are the leader who is treating them like partners. You are involving them in your thinking. You are giving them a say. You are sharing a stake in the venture.

Once they feel this from you and trust it, they will take ownership of what happens. They will want the plan to succeed. They will get it done. Sharing your goals and plans will help make sure they are achieved.

> Constant improvement is better than delayed perfection.

Perfect goal-setting is not required

Goal-setting is really a process, not an event. It takes time to both set and achieve goals! But rest assured, the better you get at goal-setting, the more your business will achieve its potential.

As always, the more clearly defined your goals are, the more likely you will achieve them.

Consider these words of wisdom:

> *"Success is the progressive realization of predetermined, personal, worthwhile goals."*
> —Earl Nightingale

Another benefit from having SMART goals is that it attracts the cream of the crop. Talented, motivated people want to work for leaders who know where they are going.

This motivates top quality people to join your team, which speeds you toward your goals even faster!

Customers and clients also want to do business with those who have a purpose and a plan. They can see your growth and commitment to them, and that's part of their customer experience with you.

Remember, constant improvement is better than delayed perfection. No one is a perfect goal-setter. Enjoy the clarity and confidence that SMART goals bring as they empower you to take action on your future!

THINKING: PART #4

—THE PLANNING SYSTEM TO REACH YOUR GOALS

Most business leaders know what they want but are just not sure how to get there. In my experience in consulting business owners, I have found many of them spent more time planning a week-long vacation than they did on their business.

In athletic competition, the team with the best game plan usually wins. For entrepreneurs, the best business plan will achieve success at the highest possible level.

The best business plans are easy to understand and act upon. The best business plans can be reduced to a single page.

I like to use the 1-3-5 GPS Planning System. It's like a GPS guidance system. It gets you where you want to go.

> 1-**G**oal (your goal)
> 3-**P**riorities (strategies to reach that goal)
> 5-**S**teps (steps you take for each priority)

It's a way to approach any challenge, unlock any opportunity, a way to begin with the end in mind, and it works in a one-hour meeting, a business planning session, or a short-term problem-solving task.

What would be the 1-3-5 for us to increase our sales? What would be the 1-3-5 to increase enrollment in a program? What would be the 1-3-5 to reduce drugs in your school?

Whatever the goal, apply the 1-3-5!

It's more than a system. It's a way to think. It provides foresight and insight. It helps you take action.

It unlocks creativity. It creates clarity and focus. Everyone knows what you are doing. All are focused. It invites participation and ownership. It brings synergy. It is a proven effective tool for entrepreneurs and leaders.

You introduce this 1-3-5 methodology in any venture and you are instantly the leader!

Consider this truth:

> *"The ability to plan is the master key*
> *to all meaningful success."*
> —Hal Geneen

How it works

To make the 1-3-5 GPS Planning System work for you, remember these key points:

- Work in three phases. Do the 1, then the 3, and finally the 5; finish each before the next
- First brainstorm a list of choices and then decide on the best to use
  - Don't worry about perfection; just get it done as best you can for right now
  - You can always edit and refine it later

Now comes the actual steps to apply the 1-3-5 methodology.

Step 1: the ONE goal

Naturally, you want to have one goal to shoot for, the one most important measureable outcome you want to accomplish. Most likely, however, you have several general goals bouncing around in your head or on your list. It's good to have at least three to work with, but no more than five.

As you work on this goal, remember that it should be specific and measurable with a timeline (by a certain date). It should be SMART. With that in mind, pick the one goal you really want to pursue now. Which of your general goals is the most appropriate or comprehensive?

> Most likely you have several goals bouncing around in your head. That's fine. You need at least three, but no more than five.

Perhaps the goal you choose is to increase your company profits to $200,000 by the end of the year. That is indeed specific, measurable, and with a specific deadline.

Step 2: the THREE priorities

This step is to clarify the strategies or sets of actions that will most likely lead to the accomplishment of your goal.

Make a list of the action-oriented priorities, at least five but no more than eight, that you need to take to reach your goal. Then refine that down to the three that you believe will be most effective.

The key factor to answer is this: What can you do to lead you to the accomplishment of your goal?

Select the three priorities that are most effective right now. If you are working to increase your company profits to $200,000 by the end of the year, then perhaps your 3 priority actions steps would be: 1) Increase lead generation to have 20 appointments per month, 2) Increase effectiveness of the presentation so you get 50% of the leads converted to a sale, and 3) Control costs so you have $0.40 of every $1 of revenue left over as profits.

Step 3: the FIVE steps

This is where you clarify the specific things you can do and the steps you can take to make each of the three priorities you outlined come to pass.

For each priority, you will want to create eight to ten steps you can take, and then refine that down to five steps you will commit to do per priority.

Here is a practical example, based on the goal of increasing your company profits to $200,000 by the end of the year, that shows the 1 goal, the 3 priorities, and the 5 steps:

The 1 is the GOAL:
> Increase profits by $200,000 by end of year

The 3 are the PRIORITIES:
> a. Get more appointments/month
> b. More effective sales presentations
> c. Control costs

The 5 are the STEPS:
> Get more appointments/month:
> 1. Create database of past clients
> 2. Communicate 2x/month
> 3. Articulate value proposition in a

compelling way so they want to buy
4. Make offers they would respond to
5. Add 10 people per week to database

More effective sales presentations:
1. Go through selling procedure, ask the right questions, identify what they want to accomplish
2. Add testimonials for credibility
3. Practice sales presentation 30 minutes per day
4. Take sales presentation to local meetings and ask for referrals
5. Track what comes in, appointments, and who wants to work with you

Control costs:
1. Make sure your budget is in place and each area is tracked
2. Share ideas with each other on how to reduce costs
3. Track performance per month
4. Reward people with $50 certificates for cost-saving ideas
5. Every month you are on track, host a company celebration

Apply 1-3-5 to every goal

The 1-3-5 GPS Planning System is a thought process that takes time, focus, and effort. You really have to think hard about it and work it. You have to make decisions which become commitments.

At first it may seem cumbersome, like a new skill it

takes time to learn. Rest assured that it gets easier with practice and use. Soon you'll start to do it mentally and quickly.

The end results are worth it because this process always produces improvement and often it generates amazing results. That is a Return On Investment that you can take to the bank!

THINKING: PART #5

—FOUR BUSINESS MODELS TO GROW YOUR BUSINESS

Whatever your business, you are looking for growth, increased performance, and long-term success. Understanding these four models, and operating accordingly, can put profits where they need to be – in your pocket!

Model #1: Craft your **economic model**

Your economic business model explains how your business uses its assets (people, systems, things) to bring in revenue. Start with defining what you offer:

Products
- single purchase?
- multiple purchases?
- how often do they purchase?

Service
- One-time fee?
- Ongoing fee?
- Multiple services offered?

Both
- Product needs maintenance
- Monthly/annual commitment

Look for opportunities to create recurring revenue for stability and dependable revenue stream. Here are some examples you could implement:

- Multiple purchase discount
- Monthly subscription for unlimited services/support
- Various packages: Gold, Silver, Bronze

Once you have options for purchasing at different levels and packages, have a billing system to bring the revenue to you (i.e. Freshbooks).

Model#2: Set up your **lead-generation model**

You will need to create a system that allows you to identify, locate, attract, and contact a steady stream of people who want what you have to offer. This is accomplished by implementing a Customer Relationship Management (CRM) system that consistently builds a client database, communicates with it, and gets repeat and referral business from it.

> **The key is to systematically and consistently add new names and contact info to your list. Always!**

The foundational key is to systematically and consistently add new names and contact information to it every day.

How did clients make contact with your business? Were they referred? Can you repeat it? Where are you currently getting new contacts from? What other sources can you use?

 My company has developed a technology tool called Next Level Suite www.NLSuite.com to build campaigns to communicate consistently with your contacts. You can build targeted messages to different types of contacts (i.e. those who have never purchased, those who have purchased once, and those who have purchased multiple times).

You will want to track statistics on the effectiveness of your communications.

- How long does it take to convert someone?
- How many leads were converted to customers?
- How many customers referred you to someone else?
- What campaigns received the most responses?

Model #3: Establish a **budget model**

Once you have created an economic model for your business and have your lead-generation system starting to take shape, it's time to create a budget.

What are your expenses each month? What are your income expectations?

Use a profit and loss (P&L) statement to continually monitor your budget weekly or, at a minimum, monthly. You will need to make adjustments to your business based on actual, not projected, budget numbers (actual expenses and actual revenue). Find a tool or system (i.e. Quickbooks) to automate the process.

Keep it simple at first. As you grow, your financial system will be more developed. The key is to have your budget and Profit & Loss statement in place ASAP!

Model #4: Clarify your **organizational model**

An organizational chart is a diagram that shows the

structure of an organization as well as the relationships and relative ranks of positions. This type of chart can help you see which current positions are needed, which will assist with planning for the future.

After all, you are the one who needs to know how many people you will need, when you will need them, and the skills and experiences they will need. It involves asking such questions as:

- What is the current structure of your organization?
- What is the desired structure of your organization?
- What structure will best support your goals?

To get started, you will need to list all the tasks and functional areas you need, such as sales, marketing, manufacturing, etc. Then create job titles for each functional area. Finally, build each functional area, starting from the bottom and working up.

When these four foundational models are in place, your business is on very solid ground.

Thinking Summary

- The High Achiever says, "What needs to be done and how can I do it?" The Entrepreneur says, "What needs to be done and *who* can I get to do it?"
- Constant improvement is better than delayed perfection
- A business plan doesn't need to be an overwhelming process. The most effective can fit on one page.
- Know your numbers.
- Creativity comes after you master your models. Keep it simple!

- Your database is your business. Feed it daily!

CHAPTER TWO

TARGETING

What you seek is what you will find.

You can only hit the target you are aiming at.

With your business, knowing what your target is – that's priceless!

TARGETING: PART #1

—GETTING MORE CUSTOMERS

We are all business owners and leaders, and we must find more ways to attract business. No matter how good our product or service may be, unless we have customers and clients, our venture will not succeed.

To do that, we must master the second discipline of business: TARGETING. This is all about identifying, locating, contacting, and attracting a steady stream of people who want what we have to offer.

Technically you don't exist and are out of business if you don't have any customers, so it all comes down to finding and attracting customers.

There are three kinds of customers you want:

1. new
2. repeat
3. referral

You always need new ones, especially at the beginning! And you want existing customers to keep coming back. And you want every customer to spread the word to all of their friends and send you referral business. Attracting new customers is where it starts, but using those customers wisely is where the money really begins to multiply.

Getting new customers

Now, there are two ways to get those initial new customers:

- **Prospecting:** contacting people directly (in person or by phone) and finding out if they need your product or service. You are *seeking* customers at this point. It is the most direct, cost-effective, and proven way to get more business.

- **Marketing:** sending out messages (advertising, direct mail, email, social media, promotional items, etc.) that are intended to attract customers. If what you say interests them or if what you offer appeals to them, then they will come to you. They may want more information or they may be ready to buy right now.

Prospecting	Marketing
Finding	Attracting
Time	Money
More proactive	More passive

The mistake many businesses make in the beginning is being marketing focused. At the front end of any venture you want to be prospecting focused until you have revenue to support a marketing budget.

The success of your business venture depends on your mastery of attracting, keeping, and multiplying your customers. You need new customers, you need to keep the customers you get, and then you need those customers to refer others to you.

Think of it this way – you need air, water, and food to survive, right? It's exactly the same with getting, keeping, and multiplying your customer base. Exactly the same! Without air, water, and food, it's over. Remember, we need air most urgently, then water, and finally food. New, repeat, and referral customers have a similar priority.

Creating offers

The goal of your marketing is to attract more new, repeat, and referral business. One powerful tool in effective marketing is creating compelling offers that cause people to call you, do business with you, or refer someone to you.

You can make two kinds of offers: direct or indirect.

> **Direct** means they will be directly doing business with you. They may be taking advantage of a discount or a special delivery offer (by deadline) or a special added value (i.e. two for the price of one).

> **Indirect** offers mean they will get something of value which may eventually lead them to do business with you, but not right now. These are usually offers of free information or special reports, such as an article like "The seven mistakes to avoid when hiring a general contractor," that will put you on someone's radar should they need your services later.

Be creative with your offers. Consider what prospective customers might want to know about or would want to be able to do right now. Then make your offer.

 When they respond, it means they have raised their hand and have a need for your services. This will allow you to begin building a relationship with them.

All of your marketing should include compelling offers that attract new, repeat, and referral business.

> As you need air, water, and food to survive … so you need to get, keep, and multiply your customer base!

How you must think

When it comes to your customers, you must always ask yourself these questions:

1. What is my business doing to find or attract new customers?
2. What am I doing to get my past customers to do business with me again and again?
3. What is being done that will cause all those who know me and have used me to send others to me?
4. What compelling offers can I promote?

TARGETING: PART #2

—THE IDEAL CLIENT

Target marketing is the key to your business growth. Getting clear about those whom you serve helps you identify your ideal client or the bull's eye of your target.

Your ideal clients need what you offer, benefit from what you do, and appreciate you. They can also afford to pay what you charge and feel it is worth it.

What's more, your ideal clients don't hassle you, complain, or threaten. As you serve your ideal clients, they will naturally bring you more prospects and customers who are just like them. As they say, like attracts like!

They do viral marketing for you. They provide word-of-mouth advertising about how good you are.

Do you know what your ideal clients look like? Which of your past customers were in these ways ideal? Ask yourself how they came to know you; how did they find you? Where did they come from?

Here is the question you must answer:

 Am I seeking, contacting, and communicating with the right people?

When you serve the right people, everything lines up and business grows exponentially!

Clarify your target

Target marketing is a very serious business because it can be the difference between bankruptcy and billions, survival and success. It's also incredibly fun and satisfying to know you are hitting the target.

When you consider target marketing, these are the questions you need to be asking yourself:

- Whom do I serve?
- Who needs my product or service?
- Why do they need it?
- What issues are they dealing with?
- Where are they?
- What are they looking for and where?
- How can I reach them most effectively?

The truth is your ideal clients are the very people you can serve the best. They need you – and you need them.

Knowing who your ideal clients are and what they look like allows others to help you find more of them. Not long ago I was at a networking event where I met several entrepreneurs in a one-on-one discussion. I met a woman with a direct sales business that sold skin care and cosmetic products. I asked her several questions about why she decided to partner with this company and how the products have been a benefit to her.

Because I'm a networker and want to help others make connections, I naturally asked her questions so

I could better understand her ideal client. When I asked her, "Who is your ideal client so that I will know when I spot them?" she responded, "My ideal client is anyone with skin!"

> The more focused and specific you can be, the more others will be able to help you grow your business!

It's a catchy jingle, and perhaps a phrase used to recruit people into her business, but it's a horrible way to describe your ideal client. You must be more specific than that!

The more focused and specific you can be, the more others will be able to help you grow your business.

Finding your clients

Sometimes there are certain criteria that can help lead you toward the ideal client base, which then helps grow your business.

Consider these specifics. Can you use them to help you find more of the right type of clients?

- *Socio-economics* — Can they afford you, your service, or your product? If so, are they able, ready, and willing?
- *Geography* — Where do they live? Does it matter? If you can focus on a niche market, you will dominate it.
- *Age, experience, maturity* — Do these factors make a difference at all with your clients and getting them to buy what you offer? If so, find out why.
- *Special interests and hobbies* — Are there specifics like these that will help, or hurt, you attract more clients?
  - *Education or intellectual interests* — Is your

client search affected by education or intellectual interests? If so, then you must find out how to use this to your advantage.

- **Special needs or wants** — Everyone wants and needs something. Do you know what your clients need and want? You should. That is the targeting game!

I knew of a lady in real estate who wanted to serve the higher end real estate clients. However, she didn't circulate with that type of clientele. She simply didn't live in their world, but she wanted to!

What could she do?

Admittedly, she wasn't at that level, but she decided she must do what she could do. She creatively took action.

> She didn't hang out with her intended clientele, so she joined a country club so that she could.

> She didn't dress like them, so she bought clothes that would let her blend in.

> She didn't see them very often, so she went to the country club every day. She drank soda water and ate crackers (that's all she could afford), but she was there!

> She didn't know them, so she got to know them gradually on their turf. Relationships were created. Trust was built.

In the end, she got the chance to work with a few of them as they bought or sold their homes. This led to more business, and eventually, as her business grew, she ended up buying a house in the same neighborhood as her clients. In the end, she could afford to be a full member of the country club and to buy lunch.

You know what you are looking for, so describe your ideal client and ask for those specific leads.

Knowing what your ideal client looks like will help you find them and them find you. Serving those who can afford you and who value what you do makes your work enjoyable and fulfilling, and that causes you to consistently increase the value of what you do for those you serve.

Don't waste time, effort, and aggravation on those who aren't good clients. They will try to cut your prices, they will complain, and they won't be satisfied. Let them go! Move on! Spend time finding those who want you, need you, can pay you, and appreciate you.

That increases value and worth, and that's the way it's supposed to be!

Remember, SW SW SW SW SW.

> Some Will.
> Some Won't.
> Some Wait.
> So What.
> So Who's NEXT?

TARGETING: PART #3

—NAME IT AND CLAIM IT

The skill of identifying, locating, contacting, and attracting people who want what you offer is an absolute must for your business.

You accomplish this by understanding and describing your value proposition, which is what you provide to your customers and clients.

More importantly, your value proposition clearly states the **benefits** customers receive when they buy from you. It's not the features (what the product or service *does*) that people care about as much as they care about the benefits (what they *get* and *experience* from it).

That is why the benefits are so important – and that is why communicating clearly what those benefits are is even more important!

I have the perfect bad example for you! As a young entrepreneur and new in the real estate business, I went looking for new business by knocking on doors to find people who wanted to sell their homes.

One house had a For Sale By Owner sign in the front yard. "Great!" I thought. "There is a high probability that they could be my client!"

The homeowner came to the door and I started into my presentation about how I could assist him in selling his home. I had yet to sell a home and I don't remember much of what I said, but I will never forget the first question that came out of his mouth. He asked, "Why should I hire you to sell my home versus what I am already doing?"

> It's not the features that people care about as much as they care about the benefits ... what they get!

My immediate response was to start to hand him the colorful brochures my company had equipped me with and tell him why our blue sign was better than his red and white one. I knew my comparisons were not powerful, but I didn't know how to answer his question.

He repeated, "I don't care about what color the sign is or what these stats say. Why should I hire you?"

You would think I would have prepared for this, the most obvious question, but I had no answer.

Of course I didn't get a follow-up appointment, but it was the best door I ever knocked on! Never again would I be left without a compelling answer to WHY someone should work with me and how they would benefit.

A solid value proposition will answer the following questions.

- ✓ What will you provide?
- ✓ How will the customer benefit?
    - ✓ What problem can you solve?
    - ✓ What will the customer experience?

✓ Does it compel someone to take action?

Entrepreneurs master the art of sharing their value proposition by constantly working on their words, phrases, and concepts. This is, to be precise, the specifics of how they talk about their business and what it does.

In your business, spend time forming the key words and phrases that best define your products and/or services. Here are several practical methods to discover the power words that reflect your business:

- You and your employees can brainstorm.

- Tell your story to someone and get their feedback on the themes they hear and what words reflect those themes.

- Ask your customers what they would tell someone else about your business.

- Look at what problems you solve in the market place.

- Consult the book *Words that Sell* by Richard Bayan.

Name it and claim it

Admittedly, the companies with the marketing plan that uses words and phrases that everyone seems to know or remember are the ones most likely to get the business. That's just the way it is!

Perhaps you've heard these words before or know the company that crafted these words:

- (Your company) 5 Star Service Guarantee

- (Your company) 5 Step Process
- (Your company) System for Success
- (Your company) Price Match Guarantee

Once you have it, you add your company name to it, thus claiming it as yours.

One of our Master Networks members and General Contractor, Mickey Elias, described how he used this concept to get a leg up on his competition:

> I used to give a client a bid on a project and then follow up with them a week or so later. When I had the follow up conversation, I would often be informed they had decided to work with a different contractor because their bid was cheaper.
>
> This was a serious problem. I wasn't even getting the chance to compare the bids. So I created the Elias Construction Price Match Guarantee. This states that I will match any other bid and beat it as long as it is an apples-to-apples proposal.

Through this Value Proposition, Mickey has discovered several opportunities. First, to be able to match the bid he must see the bid, thus getting the chance to save the deal. According to Mickey, most of the other bids leave off several items to make them seem lower. To the client, this seems to only create doubt in their minds about the other contractor's attention to detail.

Mickey reports that since implementing this and several other value propositions, his business has nearly tripled in gross revenue in 24 months!

Another good example is Domino's Pizza. Domino's

Pizza created the 30-minute guarantee or your pizza was free in 1984, and it helped make the company the world's largest pizza delivery company, with 5,300 locations.

Domino's scrapped the offer in 1993 due to safety concerns of the delivery drivers, but to this day, stores still receive calls asking for the offer when the pizza doesn't arrive within 30 minutes. Talk about an effective value proposition!

You are doing the same thing. You are crafting your value proposition and the key words and phrases of your business that compel prospects to do business with you.

Once you have that ready, teach everyone in your business to use these key words, phrases, and concepts. In so doing, it becomes the language of your team and everyone learns to talk about your business in a unique, exciting, and attractive way.

And news like that spreads like wildfire!

TARGETING: PART #4

—CREATING THE ULTIMATE SOUND BITE

In this fast-paced technological age, we are used to instant information. Political candidates no longer create content-rich speeches but rather quick, powerful sound bites!

Many people refer to this as an elevator pitch. (I don't know about you, but nobody usually talks when I'm on an elevator.)

Some organizations call it a one-minute commercial and they train you how to create a powerful one-minute presentation that will wow your prospects. (I've always wondered what you do if they don't have 60 seconds. "Excuse me, sir, can you stand still? I am not finished with my minute. I have more to say!")

But the point is you must be ready with a short, concise, powerful presentation that tells enough of your story so the person you are talking to gets it and can take the next step. That next step could be a sale, lead, referral, or something else that you intended.

So I created my own sound bite. I call it an "escalator pitch."

Not long ago, I was at a conference where Seth Godin, Master Marketer and best-selling author, was the keynote presenter.

 After the presentation, I was exiting the arena on the third floor to attend another training session on the first floor. As I turned the corner to get on the escalator, I noticed Seth was standing next to me. I had him for two floors!

I said, "Seth, great presentation today!"

He said, "Thank you!" Then looking at my name tag, he added, "Chas, what is Master Networks all about?"

Thankfully I have practiced my sound bite every week for several years. All that practice came down to the 20-30 seconds we had on the escalator.

> Do you have an escalator pitch?

After I shared my quick sound bite, he replied, "That sounds like a great organization! Go make your ruckus!" (Something he teaches.)

Be prepared at all times when someone asks what you do. You may only get a few seconds, so prepare and practice to quickly share who you are and what you do.

For example, I might say:

> Hi, I am Chas Wilson with Master Networks where we bring together local businesses to connect, share, and prosper. I am looking for local business leaders who are looking to grow their business by connecting to our network of business leaders.

Hopefully your sound bite will contain information that is intriguing. You want the person to ask follow-up questions and engage in a conversation.

Goal

Let's get practical. What do you expect to get from the sound bite you create?

Do you want, for example, to book one party, get two referrals, or have three people take advantage of your special offer? Or some other goal that helps strategically grow your business?

What is your goal?

Intro

You want your name, organization, and tagline to be visible, on all your publicity pieces. Use that on your sound bite as well.

Be sure your tagline is short and memorable. This is one part that you can switch up if it helps!

Your tagline should be a statement that is memorable, easy to understand, and explains your value proposition. The answers to the following questions will give you a base to start from:

- ❑ Who are your ideal clients?
- ❑ What benefits do your products and/or services provide?
- ❑ What is your value proposition?
- ❑ What makes you stand out?
- ❑ What do your customers say about you?
- ❑ What attitude do you want to convey?

Write all the answers down and look for themes and key words or phrases. Here are some thoughts on how to organize your tagline:

- • State how you are different
- • Compare yourself to your competitors
- • Use a metaphor

- Rule of Three (a triple set that describes your business)

Here are several real examples:

- A massage so relaxing, you'll say, "Ahhhhh"
- Keeping your spine aligned so it doesn't get on our nerves (chiropractor)
- More business for your business is my business (promotional items)
- Not more quality than you need, just more quality than you expect (construction)
- It's in the details (custom hardwood floors)
- Official Sponsor of the American Dream (realtor)
- Solving your business's financial mysteries (accountant)
- Get your shine on (car detailing)
- Connect. Share. Prosper. (Master Networks)

What is your unique tagline?

What you want

This is your moment! Ask for the business, and be specific and bold! This is your call to action.

> Make it easy for people to give you referrals or act on your offer by telling them exactly how they can help you.

Ask for what you want. Do you want referrals, introductions, and partnerships? Make it easy for people to give you referrals or act on your offer by telling them exactly how they can help you. Be careful that you don't over-complicate things.

Describe your ideal client. It will help you be specific in your call to action. Start by answering these questions: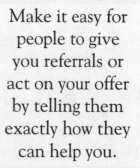

- ❑ Which of your past customers were ideal to work with?
- ❑ Why were they ideal?
- ❑ How did they find you?
- ❑ What issues did they have?

What do you need today?

Wrap Up

Conclude with your name, business name, and your tagline or slogan.

Put it into practice!

It's time to craft your full sound bite. Write it out if you have not done so.

Once your sound bite is written down, practice it over and over until it flows off your tongue when you are asleep!

You will need to plan and create separate communication plans and messages for your prospects and current clients.

There is power in your words. Make it work for you!

TARGETING: PART #5

—YOUR DATABASE IS YOUR BUSINESS

To manage communications and contacts with your prospective and current customers, you will need to invest in a system that manages your database. Having a database of people and a system that is proactive and consistent is an integral part of finding the customers you want.

Your database should include everyone you know or want to know or could do business with you.

Do you mean friends? YES.

Do you mean family? YES.

Do you mean neighbors and community members? YES.

Do you mean other businesspeople? YES.

The more people you put in, the better. Yes, you need to get their emails and phone numbers and addresses (as much information as you can), but don't wait until you have all that information. Just begin to put people in your system and then send your messages out. They might use your service and they might not, but they will begin to tell others and those people will do business with you.

A Customer Relationship Management (CRM) system is a technology system that is fundamental to your business. Many business owners are overwhelmed with technology and choose not to invest in a system that grows their business, or they do not fully understand the benefits of such a system. Neither is an excuse not to have a database.

I know that some systems are expensive and difficult to use. If you are looking for a simple, inexpensive technology system for your business, here is the one I prefer.

Actually, I helped design it and have made it available to my associates. It is very user-friendly. It's called Next Level Suite (www.NLSUITE.com). Use Promo code "book" to receive a special discount that is just for my readers.

Feed it daily

The foundational secret to this CRM database system is to systematically and consistently add new names and contact information daily. As you meet new people, collect cards, and people are referred to you, store this information in your database. Create automated follow ups and campaigns to regularly communicate with your database. These communications should be creative, personal, and have direct calls to action.

The beauty of an automated system like this is that it never calls in sick, never calls in late, doesn't take a day off, and doesn't talk back! It is the most cost-effective investment in my business.

Begin with the end in mind

I recently had a home builder request a meeting to see if I would be willing to help him get his business ready to sell. He has been in business for 20 years and built over 350 homes in that time.

One of the first questions I asked him was, "Where is the information for each of your current and past clients?"

He pointed to a file cabinet and said, "It's all in there."

Imagine how many of his past clients have not had *any* communication from him in the last 20 years! You have to wonder:

- How many of them would have built another home?
- How many would have referred him to someone wanting to build a home?

Had he just stayed in consistent contact with them, his world would be entirely different. But here is the biggest loss:

> Where is the information for each of your past and current clients?

- How much more valuable would his business be if he could show a prospective buyer a database of all contacts, date of purchase, when his last communication was, all notes from previous conversations, etc.?

My advice was to get his database set up. He immediately had his assistant enter every past client and start a campaign to reach out to everyone in his database. What he understood was what he was really selling—his database. In fact he realized that this database was the most important asset of the business he wanted to sell.

There is big money in YOUR database as well!

TARGETING: PART #6

—CONVERTING YOUR LEADS

Lead conversion is the process of taking interested prospects and helping them become paying clients. This integral act of conversion is at the heart of making business happen.

Beyond the technical knowledge and skill to deliver your product or service, you must learn to help others understand why they should work with you.

If they don't know why they should buy from you, they won't! With practice, you can become a person of influence who can connect with others and get them to say, "Yes."

Here are four basic steps to follow to convert a lead: We call it the Lead Conversion A.R.C.

The Lead Conversion A.R.C.

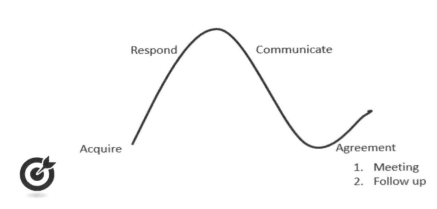

STEP #1: Acquire

A lead is someone who has inquired or has been referred to you. These are leads because you have acquired their information. At a minimum you should have a name, phone number, and email.

How will you acquire your leads? There are many sources from which you can acquire a lead. Your website, web form, email, phone calls? Face-to-face presentation? Group presentation? Referrals? All of these are sources where you can acquire a lead.

> You need a consistent, structured follow-up plan. Do you have one?

Whatever method you choose, keep it simple, for the goal is to make it easy for the prospect to know how to give their information.

STEP #2: Respond

When the lead takes action, you must respond right away.

Most of our lead acquisition sources funnel into our database. This way we can communicate with them in an automated and systematic way. This automation makes sure they are contacted or get a response immediately.

Email is the quickest way to respond and communicate. The most ideal is to connect on the phone or in person.

Think about when the last time was that you filled out a web form to request information and a real person picked up a phone to speak with you.

Have a conversation and ask about the needs they have and what problems they are facing.

This is not a one-sided conversation. Let them ask questions and share concerns. You'll be surprised how much information you will gain simply by listening.

Responding quickly step is a necessary and essential part of the process. You get to provide the necessary information that will be useful as they make their decision. At every communication, give them the opportunity to decide to meet with you or take the next step.

STEP #3: Communicate

The fortune is in the follow-up. I have learned in my business that most, if not all, of my competition fails in the follow-up. You will win or lose in the follow-up.

 Communicating is your chance to provide additional information and education. Maybe they are close to making a decision and need something to tip over the edge.

This is also a good time to share testimonials or references, as this type of third-party validation is very strong. You might even notice a certain testimony or reference that is especially impactful.

STEP #4: Agreement

As you proceed, offer support and allow them to ask questions. This is the decision point for them. Ideally you want to take the lead to one of the following two options.

1. Agree to meet with you
2. Agree to have you follow up

Agreement to meet is where you will move into your sales presentation. (I will cover the sales presentation in a later chapter.) Or the agreement is to continue to send them information, materials, or follow up at a later time.

During the lead conversion process, building trust and credibility are vital parts of your success. Represent your company, products, and services honestly, do what you say you will do, and stay focused on problem solving.

Customers love that, and when they love you, it's a done deal!

Consider what you could learn from the following example:

> Dr. Nate Bernatz recently launched his new chiropractic practice in the state to which he just moved. Not knowing anyone, he quickly started networking.
>
> Dr. Nate has a unique approach to chiropractic care that sets him apart. However, he needed to get that message out there. One of the ways Dr. Nate wanted to generate leads was to have a booth at local expo shows. So he set up a booth with a chiropractic table offering chiropractic assessments.
>
> Now here is the magic. When someone approached the booth to receive the assessment, he had to sign a short release form that allowed Dr. Nate to do his assessment.
>
> He had created a lead capture page in his Next Level Suite (www.nlsuite.com) account that listed all of the medical release information *and* asked them to put in their personal information. Then he could address their chiropractic needs and do his assessment.

The brilliance is that once they entered in their information, his Next Level Suite account took over from there. That prospective client now received an email campaign that stretched over the next 3 months. The campaign was peppered with compelling offers to come in and have an initial visit in his office. These offers had a time limit attached. Dr. Nate was able to then track that most prospects took advantage of the offer within 10 to 14 days after they started to receive his emails.

Dr. Nate reports this strategy has contributed to his quick success. He has been able to launch a practice within his first year of business that has enough clients paying monthly to support all of his expenses!

Notice how he followed the Lead Conversion A.R.C. He first acquired the prospects' information and had a system in place to respond to them. Over several weeks he communicated with them to get an agreement to meet. This simple process works!

TARGETING: PART #7

—TELLING THE STORY OF YOUR BUSINESS

Everybody loves a great story, for stories are memorable and persuasive. And as they say, facts tell but stories sell!

A good story or collection of stories can really help push your business forward. In fact:

- A compelling story will attract more business.
- Recording and remembering your story will inspire those who work with you, as people want to play a part.
- The story of your business will motivate you.

Crafting your story

Where will you tell your story? Will you put it on your menu, on your businesscard, on your website, on your wall, or somewhere else?

Your story is a powerful tool and is comprised of two important parts:

Part #1: Your story is about YOU
- What attracted you to do this?
- What did you dream about?

- How did you get started? Apprenticed? Accident?
- Who inspired or guided you? Someone who got you going?
- What did you have to learn?
- What mistakes did you make? Funny or dumb things you did? (Use humor and show you are real.)
- What interesting things happened to you? (Use details, list honors, special customers, unique things.)

Part #2: Your story is about YOUR BUSINESS
- When was it founded?
- Was it a family business? Are there family traditions?
- What happened in the early days?
- What did you do to be different? Better customer service? Better what? And what caused that "wow" experience?
- Who were your first customers?
- What challenges did the business face? What have you learned along the way? (Feel free to give embarrassing details as those can be good stories.)

Telling your story

As you tell your story, keep in mind that you want also to mention:

- What were the key moments in your growth?
- Who else in the community helped you?
- What recognition have you received? (Newspaper stories and some awards can be hung on the walls.)
- What were the most humorous or strange things that happened? (You want to add richness and tickle people's fancy.)

Keep in mind that photos and memorabilia could be a great addition to your story. Collect those parts as you grow. Do it from the very beginning. Get other people involved as well, as they would love to reminisce and tell you their memories.

Once you have written down and collected all these things, begin to craft your story in chronological order. Write it like an adventure and make it dramatic, provocative, and even outrageous. Of course, keep it positive, upbeat, and inspirational.

> People will enjoy your story because they want to connect with you and understand you better.

You may even want to use it as a blog or put it on a website or in a newsletter as you produce it. People will enjoy it, for they want to connect with you and understand you better.

When your story is written, you'll need to decide where you want to use it. You can use it in one or all of these places:

- Company brochure
- On display in your place of business
- As part of your website
- In a newsletter to your client base
- At company gatherings or anniversaries

What you have written as your story is your story until now. It is not finished, so in a year or two, you may want to add more to your story. Keep a journal and continue to collect photos, testimonials, and stories.

Your story may take on a life of its own, which is good, as it will bring in more business as a result!

TARGETING: PART #8

—CREATING A STRONG INTERNET PRESENCE

Before a purchase, most people today go online to do a bit of research, compare prices, and look for options.

That means they are checking you out before they buy from you!

Part of the research process includes getting feedback from their friends about your product or service. If they have none, then the next step is to look online for recommendations and reviews from those who have already purchased from you.

When it comes to reviews, nothing beats the power of social media! Besides providing great quality and services, you need your customers to share their experiences online! You can have your best customers share or give you a review on Google, Yelp, or other service-rating websites.

Your website

What you do, including the benefits and features, should be front and center on your company website.

Who you are is also very important for people want to know who is running the company.

 The story about your business, your history, is also vital and should be on your website. People like to understand where the company came from and other relevant details.

Your company vision and mission are also vitally important, as are customer testimonials.

You want a clear call to action (special offer, email sign-up, free download, etc.) that does something specific to increase your database and reach.

> If your future clients can't find you, the end result will probably be that they will go with someone else!

The more you post, the more videos, texts, blogs, and content by you and about you that can be found online, the higher up the food chain you will be. When prospective clients look for you or your company name online, you want to be in the top 10 or 20 listings.

If your future clients can't find you, the end result will probably be that they will go with someone else!

Social Media

Don't shy away from social media. Sure, there may be the occasional negative comment, but make sure you are engaging. Have an active voice in the conversations.

The most common platforms to think about using are Facebook, LinkedIn, and Twitter. Once you decide which platforms to use, keep these tips in mind:

- Post consistently
- Show many aspects of your business (customers, social events, community events)

- Create content that is valuable and shareable

Tell stories

If time is an issue, you may want to invest in a product like Hootsuite to manage your online brand and submit messages to a variety of social media services at the same time.

Here is one principle to consider: dominate, don't dabble. Focus on your local presence. Place links to local stories.

One of the challenges with social media is that many businesses dabble in several platforms. Gary Vaynerchuk of Vayner Media started out by dominating Twitter. He created a tremendous following on Twitter and then moved over to Facebook. For him, success came by focusing on one method at the beginning. Of course, now he has the resources to dominate multiple platforms.

You know your market and may find your ideal clients use one or two social media outlets the most. Wisdom would be to target those areas the most.

Much more can of course be said about your online presence, but do know that it is a process. Perfection isn't attained in a day!

Work toward a strong online presence, bit by bit, day by day. In time, it will be as effective and efficient as you have envisioned!

TARGETING: PART #9

—BUILD A REFERRAL-BASED ENTERPRISE

People do business with people they know, like, and respect. I'll bet that is what you do!

But here is what is even more important … people do business with people *to whom they are referred.*

That is the way we are wired. If I'm looking for a financial investor or someone to mow my lawn, I am automatically open to doing business with someone who is positively recommended. And I ask my friends and colleagues whom they recommend.

We choose to do business with people to whom we are referred, because business is about relationships. The transfer of trust through those relationships is what makes referrals so strong!

In his classic book *Endless Referrals*, author Bob Burg says that almost all decisions people make about what they buy, where they go, and whom they trust are based on referrals and relationships.

You could say it boils down to knowing the right people!

Because you intend to be that right person, your product or service should naturally bring you referrals who automatically trust you and have a positive expectation. You can't beat that!

Those referrals are ready to do business with you. On top of that, they cost less to get than any other form of advertising, marketing, or promotion.

> People do business with people to whom they are referred.

As you asked for the sale, so you need to ask for referrals. Don't be passive. Referrals will not simply come just because you do a good job. They may, but don't bet your business on it!

It is a proven fact that you will get more business from people who know, trust, and respect you if you are proactive and consistent with your efforts to get referrals.

You may want to create a referral incentive program. Here are several details to consider:

- ✓ Define what a referral is: is it any name they give you or does the referral need to make a purchase?
- ✓ Consider rewarding both the person referring and new customer being referred
- ✓ Use social media: give away something when your page reaches a certain amount of "likes" or a $5 off certificate if a customer posts about you
- ✓ Explain the rules to make it easy
- ✓ Consistently ask for referrals from current customers
- ✓ Donate to a charity for each referring customer that purchases

Growing leads is all about referrals. It's part of your process toward business growth.

 So whatever you do, put your referral program on your high priority list because it is money in the bank for you!

TARGETING: PART #10

—THE 4 C's OF THE SALES PRESENTATION

Making an effective sales presentation is one of the key skills of being an entrepreneur. Whether it's one-on-one or to a group, we must develop the ability to describe, promote, and sell our products or services.

Once you generated a lead and converted it to an appointment (as discussed in Targeting Part # 6) you now have the chance to engage in a sales presentation.

You want to lead your prospective customers to a good, mutually beneficial decision. The first thing to understand about professional selling is that it is a process. It follows a series of steps.

In fact, your prospect or buyer will go through this same step-by-step process as they are deciding whether or not to do business with you. You are merely guiding them through the buying process.

Your job is to understand the buying process well, for it is magical if done correctly. It includes these actions:

- *Knowing* your value proposition
- *Articulating* the benefits to your customers and clients
- *Understanding* how they feel

- *Following* a planned/intentional process of presentation
- *Staying* in touch with where they are

The sales process is a key part of all entrepreneurs' success. It is an extension of who they are and what they do on a daily basis. It's about working together and creating networks and relationships.

The 4 C's end result is the sales opportunity. It's a track for you to run on, a process of mutual discovery, where you and your client decide to work together. It's never just one person controlling things.

When done correctly, it's not only a beautiful thing – it's highly profitable!

The 4 C's

Selling is really the mirror image of the buying process. As a buyer, you are thinking: am I interested, does it meet a need/want, do I believe it will do it, and is the cost agreeable? If so, then you will probably buy.

It's all about the 4 C's, which are:

1. **Curiosity**: You are curious about them and you want them to be curious about you. Be interested in them. Help them get curious about you.
2. **Connection**: Ask questions to understand their wants and needs. Get a clear sense of how you can help. Convey your sincere concern for them.

3. **Conviction**: You help them become convinced that you, your service, or your product will benefit

them and meet their needs.

4. **Commitment**: You commit to doing what you said you would do. They commit to using your service and paying you for it. It's a win-win, two-way street.

Here are the 4 C's in greater detail:

PHASE #1: Curiosity

Get to know your prospective client and be genuinely interested. Don't fake the interest! And let them do most of the talking.

Your job is to ask open-ended questions (who, what, when, where, why, and how) that get them talking about themselves. That's why short yes or no questions are no good.

Find out how they ended up in this business. Show you care. If they sell computers, ask questions that relate to what they offer. Craft questions around what they do and provide.

> Get to know your prospective client ... don't fake the interest!

As you listen carefully, take notes or record the conversation. Capture as much of their information as quickly as possible.

You also want to get them to be curious about you as well. Saying things like "I am excited to ..." or "I'm committed to ..." or "If there were a way ..." enables them to understand what makes you tick. You are dropping hints and pushing things forward in the sales process, but you are also helping them to know you better.

Asking questions like "If there was one thing I could do to help grow your business, what would it be?" poses a strong curiosity-based question that everyone in business will want to answer. And if you can meet that need, then they will probably let you try.

Curiosity is about you being interested in them and them being attentive to you. It's about you asking great questions and listening to the answers. It's about getting to know each other, gaining rapport, and building trust.

That is a perfect foundation!

PHASE #2: Connection

As you ask questions about their business, work, and challenges, you will naturally get a feel for how you can help them through your business. You are looking for their needs, wants, and issues.

Have questions (5-10) that guide them to what you have to offer. For example, a realtor might ask these questions during their conversation: "How long have you lived at that address? Where did you move from? How did you happen to pick this area? If you were to move, where would you go?" These questions let realtors know if they are needed or not, and the questions lead prospects down a specific path.

Similarly, you must determine if the people you are talking to are viable prospects for you and your business.

Connection is about coming to the understanding that there may be a good reason to do business together. Get clear on what they want and need, how your service will help them, or even if it will, and if you want to work with them.

PHASE #3: Conviction

The sales presentation formula is: feature, benefit, and feeling. The product or service you provide gives your prospects a benefit, and from that benefit comes a feeling of satisfaction! Perhaps it's the joy of saving money and using that money elsewhere.

> If there was one thing I could do to help grow your business, what would it be?

Everyone is different, but the products or services you provide don't change. The benefits to your clients will vary somewhat, depending on what motivates your clients. That's partly why you have been creating curiosity and connecting.

The benefit + feeling combination is a powerful force, so have your top benefits ready to offer. Then as your conversation progresses, pick the ones that fit the best.

If you have 5-10 top benefits, use 3-5. Don't over-talk. That will be a distraction.

After you state the benefits, show evidence that you can do what you say. This can be a demo, research, third-party endorsements, testimonials, video clip, and more.

Check for agreement at this point. Did your evidence make sense? Ask if there are any questions. You want them to be convinced at this point.

Conviction is where you describe what you do, the benefits they receive, and how it will make them feel. They become convinced that they should buy from you!

PHASE #4: Commitment

Ask for the order by saying, "Are we ready to go ahead?" or "Let's get started" or "Here's what will happen next." Be assertive. Give them the forms to sign. Be confident.

Review with them what you are going to do and the commitments you are making. This is good for them to know. Say how soon things will happen so they know your schedule.

Check for their agreement. You want to make sure nothing is in the way at this point. "Is there any reason we can't just go ahead with this?" is better to ask than "Are you ready to begin?" If nothing is in the way, then you proceed.

If hesitations or delays come up, deal with them with respect. Probe (find out more) and neutralize the concern. You don't have to overcome it or negate it. This is not the time to debate; it's a time to agree.

Then reaffirm the benefits and results they are about to receive. After they say yes, reaffirm what you'll do. Remind them.

The Commitment step used to be called "closing," but the mutual agreement to do business together is more of a lasting commitment than it is a short-term close. They commit to working with you and paying you, and you commit to doing everything you said you would do, and maybe surprising them with doing even more than that.

Summing it up

 The 4 C's of the sales presentation is an art and a skill that you learn over time. Those who prepare and practice do better than those who wing it.

Prepare notes for the conviction step, features, benefits, results, and feelings. Do this exercise and pick the best and most appropriate points to discuss.

Then prepare the evidence: facts, research, endorsements, testimonials, and success stories. Use visuals where appropriate.

> You are building for a long-range, trusted, referral-generating relationship!

Don't be too formal. That will give an awkward feel to everything. You want to be more conversational in tone. Of course, make it comfortable and easy to follow!

Practice the 4 C's of selling daily. Do it as a creative mental exercise, rehearse it by yourself, practice it with others, and put it to work in your business.

Preparation is necessary in creating a selling process that is comfortable, customized, and effective.

> **Product:** Know your products – all of them. How will your products benefit the client? Customize the products you share to fit the specific problem.

> **People:** Who have you been successful helping in the past? How might past successes help you with the next customer? Who could be a reference or give a testimonial for you?

> **Passion:** Remind yourself why you love what you do. What excites and motivates you to go to work every day? Get yourself in a positive mindset.

Lastly, after every sales presentation, capture all of the information you have on that person. Record it on a digital recorder or on a voice mail system.

Verbally recall all the specifics you learned about them (business, names, spouse, work, kids, interests, education, hometown, etc.)

The longer you wait, the less you will remember. Write it down or get it recorded. Then have someone transcribe your recording and put the information in your CRM database. It will be there for you to review before you meet them again.

You are, after all, building for a long-range, trusted, referral-generating relationship! That is what TARGETING is all about.

Targeting Summary

- Ask for referrals, service them well, and say, "Thank you!"
- Successful Entrepreneurs invest the time and resources in building a strong database.
- My ideal client respects me, wants what I provide, and is excited to pay for it.
- Professionals practice and prepare their sales presentation.

CHAPTER THREE

TRACKING

How do you know if you are on track?

Do you know what expenses are eating you alive?

Better yet, do you know what business steps you are taking that are getting you a great Return on Investment?

It's time to know, now!

TRACKING: PART #1

—THE FINANCIAL MINDSET

All top performers keep track of how they are doing. Professional athletes, performing artists, and successful entrepreneurs track their performance and their progress.

Great business leaders are trackers. They know what is happening in their businesses, they record and measure performance, and they know their numbers. This allows them to understand what is working and what is not.

What you pay attention to and get feedback on will improve. That is the magic of feedback and why tracking is the third business discipline.

The financial mindset you need

It all begins with an understanding and sense of the value of money. One outcome of the business, one of the key numbers to track, is profit. Let's be clear that profit is really the result or goal but not the purpose of the business.

It was once said, "Profit is no more the purpose of business than eating is the purpose of life." Read that carefully.

The lesson is that we don't live to eat, but eating provides us the health, energy, and sustenance in order to lead a productive, purposeful life.

Profit is not the purpose. The business is not defined

by its profitability. It is more a measure of the success of the business or the financial health of the business, not its purpose. The purpose is what it delivers, who it serves, and how others benefit from the work. Both the customer and the employees benefit from a purpose-driven business.

So we understand that keeping track of profit is a measure of the health of the business and it is important to have a healthy business.

Money increases your impact

In my years of training and consulting many business owners, I have discovered we all have different relationships with or views of money. How we look at it is vastly different. Some grew up very poor and have even developed a sense of guilt toward the profit their business is creating.

Creating a successful business that produces profits will provide you with the ability to fulfill your purpose. Money is the great revealer. If you are a kind and giving person, then having more money will only provide you more opportunities to do so.

> Money is the great revealer … if you are a kind and giving person, then having more money will only provide you more opportunities to do so.

My friend and business mentor has done very well financially because he created a strong business. Most people are not aware of how well he has done and how this has served his purpose in life, which is that of serving others.

I have personally witnessed him help many people

with car repairs, rent payments, food on their table, and more. These kind acts of service have for the most part gone unnoticed by others. Of course, he is not doing it for any recognition.

This money or profit from his business served his purpose and was truly a blessing and benefit to him and many others.

TRACKING: PART #2

—KNOW YOUR ECONOMIC AND BUDGET MODELS

Here is the key to how I look at my budget. My budget is the way I predict and forecast my intentions for the business over a period of time. It is not just an administrative or clerical aspect of my business. It would be a mistake to view it that way.

I see myself as an investor in my business, holding my money accountable. I do this by having a budget and tracking my actual spending and comparing it to the budget.

In the early days of the business, I was the one who put the budget together and tracked the income and expenses. Eventually we could afford to hire a bookkeeper who could enter those in to a program like Quickbooks.

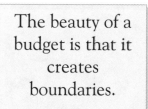

The beauty of a budget is that it creates boundaries.

Hiring a bookkeeper allowed me more time to work *on* the business and now spend my time reviewing the numbers.

The beauty of a budget is that it creates boundaries. Many business owners ask me if they should spend their money on this or that. My response is always the same: "What does your budget say?"

That usually answers the question quickly.

Those of you reading this book will be in many different industries and your budget models will vary. As you build a budget, one good rule of thumb for most is a breakdown that looks something like:

Income
-Cost of Sale
-Expense
=Net

Cost of sale is simply anything that costs you money at the time of a sale. For example, if you pay a commission on a sale to someone, then that would be a cost of sale because you only pay when a sale is made.

Expenses are everything else that is a fixed cost each month, and controlling your expenses goes a long way in giving you an advantage over your competition.

I meet with my team every month to review our budget and determine where we need to reduce expenses, re-allocate funds, and forecast future spending.

TRACKING: PART #3

—THE KISS FORMULA

The KISS formula for business has been around for ages. Some consider it to be Keep It Simple Stupid or Keep It Simple Superstar. Whatever you call it, the point is always the same:

> Keeping things simple means they are more likely to get done correctly.

Sadly, it seems to be our human nature to complicate things. That is why many entrepreneurs and business leaders do just the opposite. They make things more complicated than they really need to be, and that slows things down and increases costs.

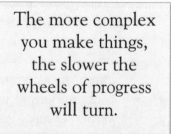

The more complex you make things, the slower the wheels of progress will turn.

If you question this fact, consider the government's documents that are hundreds and thousands of pages in length. How can you ever do anything correctly, effectively, or efficiently if you have to wade through the paperwork! Clearly, it's never going to happen. The best entrepreneurs and business owners keep things simple.

On a practical level, are you doing that in your business? Perhaps you are following the wrong models. Or maybe you are imitating businesses and ventures that are much bigger than yours and their required complexity is not required for you.

I have found that some business advisors (attorneys, CPAs, marketing professionals, etc.) have been educated to use and recommend complex systems. However, for most small businesses, the complexity makes things more confusing and harder to do.

Less gets done and costs go up. How's that going to help your business grow?

KISS everything!

When you put a new system in place, start with basic, simple, and easy to use. Always start there.

For example:

- Your initial financial ledger and monthly Profit and Loss statement only needs to have a few categories.
- Your production tracking system (leads, appointments, and sales) only needs to have a few key numbers.
- Your customer database (CRM) only needs to contain a few key data fields and be able to perform just a few communication functions.
- Your marketing message needs to be simple and basic: a warm, personal greeting, one interesting fact that is about your business (or one simple testimonial) and an offer of service.

When you make things complicated, you also make them harder to do and easier to put off doing. Procrastination suddenly becomes an attractive option!

 Instead, put the right systems in place, keep them simple, and get them working – now! You can add complexity later when the business gets bigger. I should add IF it's even necessary. It probably isn't!

Here are a few suggestions of things to Keep Simple:

- **Budget**: At a minimum, review monthly. Track your actual expenses and income against what was forecasted. Make adjustments as needed if income is coming in lower than forecasted.

- **Billing**: Use a system to ensure billing is automated (ie: Freshbooks). If automatic payments are being collected, ensure your bank account is reflecting those deposits.

- **P&L**: Use Quickbooks, another automated system, to track financials and pull reports to stay current on your business.

- **Production**: Use a spreadsheet to track leads, appointments, and sales.

Keeping things simple means you get things done correctly, faster and faster! As they say, if it isn't broken, don't fix it.

I say, keep it simple, because if you complicate things, you will break them!

TRACKING: PART #4

—THE SEVEN KEY NUMBERS

High-achieving entrepreneurs keep track of how well they are doing. On a practical level, it means that you need to record what happens, measure your performance, and know your numbers. As a direct result, what you measure will improve. What you watch gets better.

How does tracking help? To begin with, tracking the numbers of results, performance, etc. helps you to:

- understand what is and isn't working
- hold yourself and others accountable
- make smart and timely changes

The numbers to track

Accountability begins with counting. This isn't about tracking any old number. Not at all! This is about tracking the very numbers that build the foundation to your success. These numbers will make or break you.

There are seven numbers that a business entrepreneur pays close attention to and tracks:

1. Leads
   2. Appointments
   3. Sales
   4. Customers in your database

5. Income
6. Expenses
7. Profit

Very interestingly, these seven numbers divide naturally into three distinct categories. These categories are the pillars of success in any business venture:

#1) Productivity
- Leads
- Appointments
- Sales

#2) Growth
- Customers in your database

#3) Profitability
- Income
- Expenses
- Profit

Tracking is an essential part of your plan for business growth and expansion. And over time, you will begin to see trends and know if you are on track to meet your prospecting and productivity goals.

In most businesses, income, expenses, and profit need to be tracked on a weekly or daily basis. Except for staying within the budget, most small businesses will do very well to simply look at the three financial numbers on a consistent monthly basis.

The more you know your numbers the better your business will perform. Are you getting the numbers you need to take your business to where you want it to go? Are you doing better than last month or better than this month last year? Are you on track to hit your production and financial goals for the year?

The number of contacts in your database is the most important number to track and to grow. You must put systems in place to both capture contact information as well as communicate with those contacts about your services, products, benefits, special offers, and a way to send you referrals.

There are many ways to track your prospecting, productivity, and database increase. I suggest a simple Excel document, which would look something like this:

	A	B
1		**TOTALS**
2	**Productivity**	
3	Leads	0
4	Appointments	0
5	Sales	0
6		
7	Growth	
8	Customers in Database	0
9		
10		
11	**Profitability**	
12	Income	0
13	Expenses	0
14	Profit	0
15		

These numbers predict and determine your future. Strangely, entrepreneurs often disregard this.

Careful tracking = greater Return On Investment

The most successful, fastest growing business owners put their focus on the database number. As a result, they know:

- how many people (including past customers, current prospects, and community advocates) are in their contact management system
- how many people have been added this week or this month
- how many times and in what ways these people have been sent messages or promotions or offers
- which of these people have sent them referrals

Can you do the same for your business? Do you know those numbers?

When you do, you'll be amazed at what you see, understand, and expect. For example, if you know that the jar you place in that restaurant to collect business cards is generating good leads, then you will also know you should get several more restaurants involved.

> If you aren't tracking, how can you know what works?

Do what works! But if you aren't tracking, how can you know what works? Conversely, if what you are doing isn't working, how will you know if you aren't tracking?

Your growing database of names, addresses, phone numbers, and email addresses is one of the most important assets of your business. Everyone on your team should be adding people constantly to your database. What's more, every contact with a customer or potential customer should result in an addition.

Once you have them captured, it is time to communicate with them. You can convey your services, products, and benefits, make offers, and ask for referrals. This increases your momentum and financial strength. Your database IS your business!

I have found over the years that:

> What you inspect will perform better than what you expect.

> What gets measured gets done and what you watch gets better.

That is why you track! It's all about your bottom line.

TRACKING: PART #5

—REDUCE EXPENSES

In his insightful book *Made in America*, Sam Walton gave all entrepreneurs some pretty powerful advice when he said:

> "Controlling your expenses is always a competitive advantage."

Walton knew if you ran a business leaner and meaner than the competition, you have a very good chance of beating them because they are probably NOT controlling their expenses.

A focus on controlling expenses makes you much more aware of what is happening, how limited resources are being used, and what is bringing the greatest productivity and profit to you and your business.

Tracking gives you the edge

The key to financial management is first to keep track, to know what is happening with the money every month, eventually every week, and for some bigger businesses, every day. Your cost control skills sharpen over time and experience, which gives you the edge!

It goes without saying that you must be aware of your expenses. To not be aware is usually one step away from financial ruin. But beyond a general awareness, it is vital that you ask yourself:

"What are my three biggest expenses?"

These are the three costs that chew up most of your money. Have you considered how much of your budget is taken up by these three areas of expense?

Those three biggest expenses are almost always more than 50% and can be as high as 90%!

Start this process by looking at your top three costs and what percentage of your budget these costs represent. Perhaps it is staffing, occupancy, advertising, promotion, inventory, capital equipment, or technology. Those are common costs that are often in the top three, but your business may be unique.

Control your biggest 3 expenses

Once you know your top three expenses, focus on them. Take time to consider:

- How can they be reduced?
- Is it possible to get discounts from suppliers?
- Can you pay less up front?
- Could you buy used or discounted?
- How can you get more for less?

If you control the biggest three expenses, the rest will likely take care of itself and you will immediately be more competitive, more productive, and more profitable.

 A focus on controlling expenses makes you, an entrepreneur, more aware of what is happening. You learn how your limited resources are being used and what is bringing the greatest productivity and profit.

Use your tracking spreadsheets consistently. This will sharpen your financial skills and you will begin to look more critically at cost control.

Every dollar saved is another dollar you can put toward growing your business, and that's the way it's supposed to be!

Increase your revenue

There are three ways you can increase revenue:

1. Increase the number of clients.
2. Increase the value of each transaction.
3. Increase the frequency of transactions per year.

Most business leaders and entrepreneurs have incremental growth because they focus on adding more clients. This seems logical but can be a huge mistake.

Let me demonstrate with the following example:

EXAMPLE 1
Number of clients x Price/Transaction x Transaction/yr = Total Income (i.e. 1000 x $200 x 1 = $200,000)

EXAMPLE 2
If you only focus on the increase of clients year after year by just 10% it would look like this:

Number of clients x Price/Transaction x Transaction/yr = Total Income (i.e. 1100 x $200 x 1 = $220,000)

Your total annual revenue has increased by 10% or $20,000!

EXAMPLE 3
Imagine if you focused on increasing all three by just 10%.

Number of clients x Price/Transaction x Transaction/yr = Total Income (i.e. 1100 x $220 x 1.1 = $262,000)

By increasing each multiplier by just 10% you have increased your total annual revenue by 33% or $62,000!

Imagine if you doubled each multiplier to 20%, it would bring your total revenue increase to $124,000!

Recurring revenue

One challenge to most businesses is creating predictability in terms of revenue. For a long time my income charts looked like a roller coaster; some months were amazing and others not so great. The challenge for me was that I had to be a master of not just cash management but also forecasting.

Many industries have revenue models that existed as a one-time sale of specific product or service. Think of how you used to rent a movie. For years you would pay to rent a specific movie or buy a particular DVD. Then companies like Netflix came along and changed the revenue model. In fact, they didn't just change their own model, but they actually helped change the entire industry.

Today, when you subscribe to Netflix, you pay a monthly fee and get an unlimited amount of movies you can view. The reason this revenue model works is because they created more value for what you spend. In return, this created a predictable revenue model for Netflix. A specific number of customers x monthly subscription fee = total monthly revenue for Netflix.

This kind of model also allows the customer a low

barrier of entry to try the product. On the flip side, it also allows the customer an easy way out. Netflix experienced this as well, so they had to pivot and improve services.

One of my favorite books on this concept is *The Automatic Customer* by John Warrillow. In his book, John discusses nine subscription models that can help any business navigate the process of creating monthly recurring revenue.

> Have you created predictability in your revenue?

Looking for a way to add a recurring revenue stream to your business can add a long-term predictability to your economic model.

TRACKING: PART #6

—WHY FEEDBACK TRULY IS PRICELESS

It has been said that feedback "is the breakfast of champions." All high performers keep track of how well they are doing. They record what happens, measure their performance, and know their numbers.

What you measure and pay attention to has a way of improving. That is the magic of feedback!

Feedback comes from two directions:

1. From the TOP (what others are saying)
2. From the BOTTOM (what your products and services are saying)

Feedback from the TOP

Feedback from the top is all about customer service. Amazon has figured this out. They have built an online shopping empire and a massive market share that no one thought was possible. It isn't their prices or even their fast delivery that has created it. They have done one thing really well: track customer feedback.

 Their commitment to customer satisfaction has paid off. Jeff Bezos, Amazon's founder, says that pleasing the customer is his number one goal, even ahead of profitability.

All business owners can copy the lesson of his success. If they want customer loyalty, repeat business, and referrals all they have to do is assure customer satisfaction. And the way you do that is the same way that Bezos has – just ask your customers! Amazon asks for customer ratings on ALL transactions and about all products. If there is a customer complaint, they respond quickly and get it resolved.

> What good is feedback if you don't apply it?

Some experts in customer service say that making a mistake and resolving it quickly may build more customer loyalty than doing it right the first time. In any case, for the business owner who cares about the future, tracking customer satisfaction is critical. Do it after every business transaction. Ask how it went and what could have been done better. Keep track of your ratings. Improve them.

Don't be afraid of criticism or negative evaluations. Respond to them and take care of them. Better to know now than to never know why they didn't come back or why they didn't recommend you. Customer feedback will guide you; make your business stronger and lead to ever-increasing referrals of new business.

TOP feedback leads to accountability

What good is feedback if we don't apply it? That is what makes accountability so powerful. It's taking truth, in the form of feedback, and having the guts and determination to apply it in a way that improves performance, generates better results, and creates personal satisfaction.

That's a win-win! It is not a whip or a threat. It is a gift, one we can give ourselves and one we can offer to others. Accountability is the key to ownership of an activity, endeavor, or business.

There is a lot of talk in the world of business about accountability, but usually it's about how to hold others accountable, particularly our employees. It has a disciplinary tone to it, such as "I'm going to hold them accountable" or "I'm going to call them on the carpet."

All of this misses the purpose of accountability: mutual growth!

That's why accountable people are the ones who say, "If it's to be, it's up to me." They don't play victim and they don't look for excuses. If they mess up, they fess up. They don't just apologize; they take ownership and make it right. When good things happen, they take credit and feel good because they know they made it happen.

The way to use accountability in business is to understand where the word comes from. At its core is the word "count" or "account," which simply means that to be accountable is to keep track of things. It means you measure what happens, you face up to that and learn from it, it means that you use it for what it is – feedback!

Feedback from the BOTTOM

Feedback from the bottom is all about listening to the impact your products and services are having on your customers. This is the tracking of the small details, the business "insider information" that shows you what works and what doesn't work.

It's feedback from within! It's feedback from the bottom that helps you know what is working and what is not working. This allows you to hold money and people accountable for results and to make smart and timely changes in your business strategies and tactics.

Let me ask you a few quick questions:

- What are the key measures in your business?
- How do you determine good practices or effective performance?
- When do you review those numbers?
- How do you know when it is time to make changes?

These are the questions that help you master the tracking discipline. Again, it's not just irrelevant data we are talking about here. Far from it! This is the lifeblood of your business, and if you are getting good feedback, it will give you the clarity you need to take your business to the next level!

> Tracking the key numbers and asking for feedback will give you all the necessary information to make any changes or improvements.

Tracking the key numbers and asking for feedback will give you all the necessary information to make any changes or improvements.

The thing about change is that it rarely comes too early, rather most implement change too late or out of necessity.

By tracking and asking for feedback you will increase your odds of making the necessary improvements because you can. Information is power!

Tracking Summary

- Money is the great revealer.
- Feedback is the breakfast of champions!
- What you measure gets done and what you watch gets better.

- Your budget will create boundaries. Recurring revenue will create predictability.
- Your business is not defined by its profitability.
- Track the seven key numbers and keep it simple.

CHAPTER FOUR

TIMING

We all have the same amount of it.

How we manage it is a deciding factor in our success.

It is TIME … and how you take care of what you have each day will show the world what you are made of!

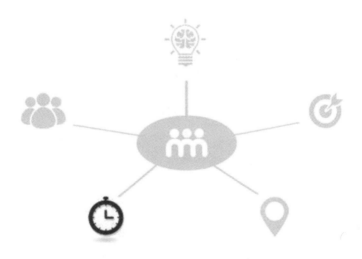

TIMING: PART #1

—THE DISCIPLINE OF TIMING

One of the biggest challenges for entrepreneurs is time management. You and I wear many hats. We have so many things to get done and have so many others who want a piece of our time. There is always more to do than you have the time to do.

It is about developing good time management practices throughout our business and teaching the right habits for everyone in the business.

To succeed as business leaders, we must master the fourth discipline: TIMING.

TIMING: PART #2

—TIME MANAGEMENT FOR ENTREPRENEURS

The Discipline of TIMING is more than just time management. Managing your time is part of it, but it is more about developing the skills, systems, and standards that allow you to get more done in less time.

Please understand that everyone struggles with time management at some level. Mastering the discipline of TIMING is a life-long endeavor. It is about progress, not perfection. In doing some things, we will have to leave some things undone.

However, the *way* you use your time will determine the success of your business.

The framework of timing

In Stephen Convey's best-selling book *The Seven Habits of Highly Effective People*, the first three habits are about being productive and effective. Simply put, they are:

#1 — Be Proactive

Be proactive means just that, be active. Actively calling, emailing, speaking to prospects, networking, and focused follow up are tasks that are being proactive.

Staying proactive helps me feel positive and fulfilled at the end of a day. It is so easy to get trapped in emails and social media during the day and not realize how much time was wasted.

> Is what I'm doing now an income-producing activity?

For many years I had a postcard hanging right above my computer screen that read, "Is what I'm doing now an income-producing activity?" It was a simple reminder to make sure I was focused on being proactive.

#2 — Begin with the end in mind

When you are clear about where you are going and what it looks like, then it is easier to decide what to do with your time. Once something is clear to you, you can make it clear for others.

#3 —Do first things first

Stepping back to evaluate what is top priority, and then doing it, is the sign that you have a keen sense of timing. For example, most sales people do their phone prospecting right away in the morning when they are sharp. Using this strategy, nothing else has the chance to get in the way.

Your time, your way

I have come to believe that the successful use of time is the ability to use time in your own way. That is because if you don't have your own plan, you'll be part of someone else's.

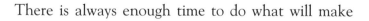

This is important to understand. Who is in charge? The answer must always be the same: you!

There is always enough time to do what will make

your business successful. That is the same for every entrepreneur in business today. That is why you must use your time in your own way. You are in charge!

Admittedly, it is easy to let others drive your schedule. Examine your situation and crank up your assertiveness if you need to. Protect your time! I work with my team to help protect my time as well. They often will help remind me when a meeting has gone too long that I need to get on to the next appointment. They will help prepare needed documents, reports, and other items for my meetings so that I can be ready.

Technology

One of my biggest time drains was the back and forth emails trying to schedule a time to talk on the phone or meet in person. I would send a few times that work for me and then they would reply that none of those work, and we would go back and forth like this for days.

I discovered a website called www.timetrade.com that allows others to connect to my calendar and schedule a meeting when I have an opening. I have control over how long meetings can be, how much availability per day, and many more. This has allowed me to take control of my day and save time when trying to schedule meetings with others.

Master skills for your time control

Every successful entrepreneur will eventually become a master of these five time-related elements:

1. **Goal-setting:** Going through the process of knowing what you want to accomplish takes time to figure out. It is of course necessary to

know where you want to go and what you want to accomplish, but setting the goal will not get you there. It's the first step in the right direction.

2. **Action planning:** There are certain steps or activities required to get you where you want to go. You set the goal, and now is the time to take the necessary steps. What those steps are, be it lead-generation, marketing, better services, more clearly defined products, more options, etc., totally depends on your goals.

3. **Outcome framing:** You need a vision for what you want the outcome to be. This applies to your goals and action steps as well as to your daily routines, such as your next meeting. Do you know what the end result is going to be for your meeting? The clearer you get, the more you envision what you want, the better it will be. Knowing what you want will help everything take a shape that is closer to what you want.

4. **Calendaring:** Can you convert your goals and action steps to your calendar? Until your goals hit your calendar, they aren't real! And until your action steps are lined up, you are not on track!

5. **Time-blocking:** Take control of your time so that you get the things done that are most important and most effective. It requires that you set aside time to do just that.

TIMING: PART #3

—BLOCKING OUT THE TIME YOU NEED

Time blocking is the technique of putting important activities on the calendar so they are not put off or neglected. This makes sure you get them done.

But to do that, you must own both the tasks and the time it takes to get them done. You are not a victim. You must lead and take ownership. That is how your priorities will get done.

Time blocking helps priorities get done! It provides adequate time for the task and assures first things first. It makes dollar-productive use of your time and places you in control.

What's more, it gains you respect and consideration. It also makes others on your team more efficient.

Power in blocking your time

Time blocking is the skill of making appointments with yourself to do high priority tasks that take focus and concentrated time. All of this is so nothing interferes with what must get accomplished.

The more you do this, the better you get at it. You will become a master at estimating time for projects as you get the jobs done. This naturally puts more money in your pockets as a direct result.

It also means fewer distractions and disruptions. You stay on task and others respect the intentionality of your efforts. Customers like this because they know you'll get the job done.

What do you time-block?

You can block off all of your time, but I would not suggest that you block off every single hour. At work, I suggest that you block off 40-50% of your time, but you'll need some flexible time for clients and responding to business urgencies.

Looking at your time, here are several things that you could immediately start blocking off:

- Time off for recreation/vacations
- Planning time to work on your business (time per week, time per year, etc.)
- Training time to learn, practice, master (meetings, etc.)
- Lead generation to gain more business (growing your business)
- Networking to build a referral-based life (part of the lead generation)
- Health for meditation, exercise, and fun
- Family to be there at the right times

Your ideal week or month plays a part. Building better habits is what you want, and since only you can judge this, the responsibility is yours to block off your time in a way that works best for you and those around you.

At work, you will want to set aside time to work on important projects and activities. For example:

 - Lead generation (making calls or developing marketing plans)

- Planning and goal-setting
- Reviewing your tracking documents
- Working on any creative project
- Meetings with key staff members

The use of time blocking allows you to create your ideal week, as we've discussed already. It ensures that all of the important tasks of your business are being worked on, your time is productive, and nothing is falling through the cracks.

The bottom line reason for time blocking:

> If you don't block time for the activities you need to get done, they simply won't get done!

> Time blocking is the skill of making appointments with yourself to do high priority tasks that take focus and concentrated time.

When you set aside time for yourself to work on important projects and activities, you are opening wide the door of opportunity!

TIMING: PART #4

—YOUR IDEAL DAY, WEEK, AND MONTH

When you study an ideal week, you will know the best time to open, close, take breaks, schedule meetings, network with clients, run email campaigns, advertise, get reports from the accounting department, send out mailers, etc. You name it, whatever needs to be done in a normal week at the office, there is inherently an ideal time in which to do it.

Note: It is called your ideal week, not your perfect week. Progress is the key.

Have you noticed:

- Banks—stay open later on Fridays.
- Restaurants—often run specials on Tuesday nights, but none on Fridays or Saturdays when they are full.
- Dentists—may offer evening hours for the busy executives who can't come during the day.
- Airlines—those red-eye flights exist only because there is a demand for them.

Imagine if everything you did in a week was done at the ideal time. That would automatically increase the effectiveness.

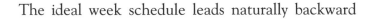

The ideal week schedule leads naturally backward

into the ideal day and naturally forward into the ideal month. The keen sense for the ideal time enables efficiency and rhythm. In time, that pace becomes a habit, and your productivity increases as a result.

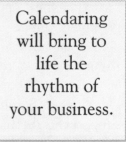

NOTE: As you work to increase your timing and efficiency, look beyond your own desk. Teach those on your team to do the same. That way they will better understand you and they will benefit from same efforts. The sooner your business reaches its ideal rhythm, the sooner you will be running on all cylinders! Finding the rhythm of your business is key to mastering your time and effectiveness. There are certain activities that will naturally happen on a routine basis, be it daily, weekly, monthly, quarterly, or annually.

Whatever the activities are, put these consistent, regular events on your calendar. This practice of calendaring will bring to life the rhythm of your business.

Why rhythm is needed

As an entrepreneur, you know that business is all about:

1. Deciding to take charge of your own actions
2. Deciding on what you want
3. Choosing your priorities

This same paradigm meshes perfectly with your efforts to manage your time. After all, you:

1. Take charge of your own time
2. Decide on what you want to spend your time on

3. Choose your priorities that are the highest and best use of your time

Finding your rhythm brings about predictability in your business for you, your employees, and your customers. This will also positively impact your personal life, as planning activities and events outside of work are easier when you have a predictable rhythm.

Developing Standard Operating Procedures (SOPs) will help support the rhythm of your business. If the processes and systems of your business are documented, others are able to continue the operation of your business in rhythm with the repetition scheduling. This frees you up to work on your business.

Put your rhythm down on paper. Use your calendar consistently. Anything that happens more than once gets a place on your calendar. Put it on your calendar if you can.

This is good for you and your team. Planning and debriefing is good practice for you and your company. Find out how something worked and apply that feedback. Also, take corrections and encouragement. It all helps create a good rhythm.

Be proactive or die

To procrastinate is to let something die on purpose, and usually that means an immediate decrease in your income or income potential. Neglecting the regular things that you must do is not an option. Never let that happen!

 Rather, be proactive. This is all about using your time effectively. It's not an obligation, but a commitment. And the sooner you can build it into your calendar, the better!

Putting something on the calendar is a disciplined move that makes you stronger and in control. You make the decision ahead of time, commit to it, and then you are the one calling the shots.

Staying proactive means if the calendar is too crowded, then you evaluate it and revise. It's your calendar, and your schedule, after all.

> Whatever gets your day off to a good start is probably the rhythm you want.

The key to your time management is the calendar. It is what brings guidance and clarity to the priorities you have set and the commitments you have made. It keeps you proactive, and that is where you must remain!

Moving from proactive to predictable

Any activity that repeats in your business, make it happen at the same time all the time. For example, if you set shipping of products to go out every Wednesday and Friday afternoon, then you put it on the calendar.

This shift from proactive to predictable is good for you, your staff, and your customers. Some companies have a meeting on Monday mornings because it keeps everyone accountable, it sets the schedule, and everything flows from there.

Whatever gets your day off to a good start is probably the rhythm you want. If you are a solo entrepreneur and have trouble getting your day going, then find out what the best way is to start your day and do just that. Perhaps you are a slow starter, then a meeting early helps you wake up and prepare.
Things you have to show up for have a way of getting you going.

Learn what works for you, and then build that into your daily schedule. Put it on your calendar.

The bottom line is of course:

Set yourself up for success!

TIMING: PART #5

—HOW TIMING HELPS YOU TREAT YOUR CUSTOMERS RIGHT

No entrepreneur would disagree with the fact that we want our customers to be satisfied and happy with our work. We want them to be "raving fans" who, in turn, refer more business to us. We want things to grow forward in leaps and bounds!

All that is normal, but maybe you are wondering, "What does timing have to do with customer satisfaction?"

Actually, they have a LOT to do with each other.

Knowing when to communicate

Customer satisfaction always includes good communication. That's a fact, for great communication means we get to know our customers, we ask good questions, and we listen to their answers. And ideally, as we've already learned, we write down their answers and refer to them in our future dealings.

With our communication, our customers know we are hearing what they need and delivering what they want. But the real secret to great customer service is timing. In other words:

> Customer service is not about how much time we spend with them, but how well we time what we do for them.

Handling expectations is a very important part of customer service. Whatever your interaction with your customers, based on their needs and the services or products you provide, make sure you are setting the right expectations.

For example, when it comes to connecting with customers, they need to know how long things will take and when they will hear back from you. Whatever times work for you, make it a specific time, such as every Monday and Thursday at 9 a.m. or Friday afternoon between 2 and 4 p.m.

> Stay ahead of the game with consistent communication and customer service timing.

You want to let them know when you are available for calls, when you will return calls, and what to do if they have an emergency and need to reach you. That will be more useful and better received than telling them you are available at any time of the day.

In every case, plan your calls to them and make those calls when you said you would. It feels much better for them to hear from you than for them to have to call you. If they haven't heard from you, that's a real problem for them!

Stay ahead of the game with consistent communication and customer service timing. Every time you communicate with your customers, make sure you are timing it right. If they call you, get back to them fast!

That will pay you huge dividends!

 Timing is sales!

At the end of the day, it comes down to sales. It

comes down to selling yourself, your goods, your products, your services, your good name, your value, and more. It's your business that you are selling!

You understand that time management is about deciding to take charge of your own actions (using time the way you want to), deciding on what you want to do (having a plan), and finally doing what is a priority (the highest and best use of your time) for you.

When you have done that, your customers will be pleased. That is what they want, and business is good when you have it in place!

Keep in mind that mastering time is a life-long endeavor. It is about progress, not perfection. As you become a better master of your time, the happier you and your customers will be. And THAT is all about customer satisfaction!

Timing Summary

- If you do not have a plan for your time, then you will become part of someone else's.
- Ask yourself, "Is what I'm doing now an income producing activity?"
- Do first things first! Time-block for priorities.
- Time is the one thing you can't get back. Be protective of your time.

CHAPTER FIVE

TEAM BUILDING

"We should not only use all the brains we have, but all we can borrow."
-Woodrow Wilson

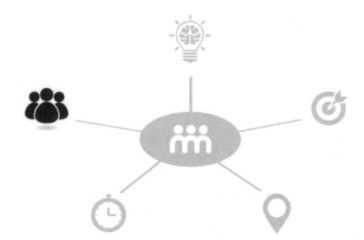

TEAM BUILDING: PART #1

—THE NECESSITY OF A TEAM

Teambuilding starts with a mindset birthed on the idea that "we" is greater than "I." Entrepreneurs often resist it if they started solo. The most common reasons for resistance are based on the following myths:

Myth 1: It costs too much!

Truth: Surrounding yourself with a team of talented people will more than likely bring about an increase in your business!

Myth 2: Creating systems to hire and train the new staff is way too complicated.

Truth: It doesn't need to be complicated at all. The following are some short, simple steps that will take the complexity out of the game.

My first hire was such a talented team member that I had him document the entire training process as we went through it. That way if I ever had to replace him or add to the team, the training was ready to go.

 Not only can you make more money in less time, but you no longer have do everything all by yourself! You are able to delegate, and that converts to more business and freedom for you.

It's better use of your time, and that saves you time and makes you more money.

Creating a team

One challenge for an entrepreneur is the fact that creating a team takes time to find people, select, train, and then manage them. Quite often, entrepreneurs struggle with the whole process of building a team.

Indeed, it can be a challenge, but entrepreneurs already possess the skills necessary to make team-building a task that can be done with speed and enjoyment!

> If your business is growing and needs to get to the next level, then you need a team!

And these principles here will also help.

In short, if your business is growing and needs to get to the next level, then you need a team! And if you need a team, then it's time to dive in and get it done.

TEAM BUILDING: PART #2

—THE PATH TO LEVERAGE

For entrepreneurs, leverage is the door of opportunity. Every veteran business owner has used leverage to get where they are today. The belief that "one person alone can do anything significant" is a myth.

Leverage means getting more done in less time with less of your own effort. It's a beautiful thing, and the sooner you embrace this concept, the faster you will get where you want to go.

Clarification needed

Many misunderstand the concept of leverage. They tend to equate business leverage with hiring people, being responsible for those people, managing them, and having to provide salaries and benefits.

Leverage is far more than responsibility, work, and management.

In business, leverage simply means getting things done through other people.

And in the simplest of terms, leverage is freedom!

The sooner you embrace the power of leverage, the faster you will get where you want to go.

 There are many ways to get leverage: training and mastery, systems and standards, tools and technology. All of these can help us get more done in less time. But the number one source of leverage for the business owner is always going to be: people!

The right people with the right talent doing the right things can cause productivity to expand and profitability to explode.

Are you ready?

A high achievers asks, "What needs to be done and when can I do it?" The entrepreneur asks, "What needs to get done and who can I get to do it?"

Almost all solo entrepreneurs or small business owners look back and wish they had added people in their business sooner than later.

> Leverage is the door of opportunity.

Here is the question that will determine your readiness:

> Am I doing things today that would be better to have delegated to someone else?

Or ask yourself:

> Could I be using my talents and skills to do things that matter more and generate greater income?

If you are a $100 per hour person doing $20 per hour work, then it's time to stop, look, and listen.

Here is what I mean:

- Stop doing that stuff!
- Look for the right person to do it!

- Listen to that inner voice that is telling you how much you will be improving your work and your life.

What phase of leverage are you in?

There are four phases of leverage:

1. Personal
2. Virtual
3. Part-time
4. Full-time

Phase #1: In the Personal Phase, you are just getting someone to do things that have been taking your time but not providing personal rewards. You don't really enjoy them and you don't get paid for them. Some examples would be: cleaning your house, doing yard work, maintaining your car, grocery shopping, and running errands. You can certainly think of others. The first phase of leverage is to get someone else to do these tasks.

> Keep looking for more ways to use these services so that you can do more of what you love to do or get paid for.

Phase #2: The second source of leverage is the Virtual Phase. You can hire services online to do all sorts of specialized things you need done. This may include answering the phone, maintaining your database, responding to Internet inquiries, doing bookkeeping, and many more. These do not require employment, and you only pay for what you use.

 Phase #3 and #4: Focus on phases one and two before you take on the hiring of more part-time or full-time employees. Keep looking for more ways to use these services so that you can do more of what you love to do or get paid for.

The next two phases of leverage involve hiring people. The right people, with the right talent, doing the right things, can cause productivity to expand and profitability to explode.

They are discussed further in the following pages.

TEAM BUILDING: PART #3

—THE PROCESS OF GROWTH

Growth of a company is like a city street in that you have neighborhoods, stores, restaurants, car dealerships, gas stations, schools, churches, etc., in some determined order. It is the order that creates flow, efficiency, effectiveness, and success. That is why you will never see a mall without parking spaces or a neighborhood with a car dealership inside of it.

Likewise, there is a process and an order of growth. Certain things happen at certain times, and all for a good reason.

When the time comes for a business to grow, it will follow a pattern. If I were to break it into steps, it would look something like this:

> Step #1: I do it, we do it, they do it
> Step #2: Define the work required
> Step #3: Look for talent
> Step #4: Build the culture

This pattern of growth is orderly, it makes sense, and it brings a great return on your investment!

Step #1 ... I, We, They

 These are the three levels of learning. You master it yourself, and then you add people and do something with them. The "I" has moved to "we." You are helping with the team, systems, etc. Finally, they do it without you. When this is fully implemented, you are removed from the day to day work. The "we" has moved down to "they." You no longer have responsibility in the day to day tasks but you now have the responsibility of a visionary leader. Vision will give the team direction and confidence.

Step #2 ... Define the work required

You know the work required for each job, but have you put the tasks and functions together? Have you defined it?

For a short period of time, entrepreneurs reach a place where they can't do it all themselves. They need to pass it on and it's a bit tough at this point.

It requires that you put the tasks and functions down on paper. You know what has to happen in your business for it to succeed, so with an analytical mindset, you need to sketch out and track all the necessary parts. What tasks are there and how do they group in functions?

> You know the work required for each job, but have you put the tasks and functions together?

This can be done with your early administration team. As you are telling them what needs to get done (i.e. how to make a call, prepare an order, open the store, etc.), they can track this and it becomes your operations manual. It's how you do business and how you get things done. Naturally, the manual grows as you grow, but it begins with you knowing and documenting the work required.

Not long ago, one of my clients hired another part-time support person. Aware that he was going through a very important part of the training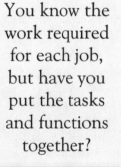

process, he had an employee create training segments on a computer that were recorded.

The new part-time employee watched it on the left side of the screen while she did the task on the right side of the screen. It was a practical training manual that was natural and easy to do.

These recorded video trainings not only taught the new person what to do, but they were perfect for the operations manual.

Step #3 ... Search for talent

Because you have defined the work required, really nailed down the job description, you know exactly who you need for your next hire. Your clearly-defined position is waiting to be filled, and that is the secret to great hiring and finding the talent you need.

Note:

> More than likely the kind of talented person you are looking for is already happily employed somewhere else. That is why he or she is TALENT!

Searching and finding talent may be the most important work of the business leader. This work may feel uncomfortable and even unproductive, but in the end it will bring stability, organization, teamwork, and profitability to your business.

It's worth doing! And doing right! I often say to take your time in this process. Be slow to hire and quick to fire.

Step #4 ... Build the culture

The last step in the process of growth is the culture that you build within your organization. I approach this not as boss or dictator, but as a head coach of a championship team. You need the best players and you need to teach them how to play at the level you want.

> On a team, there is not just one superstar. Everyone works together.

Once you have the team, then you need to get them to work together as a team. There is not just one superstar, but everyone is working together.

Mentor them personally. Help them build on what they need. You are clear on what is needed and expected, such as honesty, good customer care, positive attitude, not complaining, never talking behind people's backs, etc. That is the culture that you coach and mentor.

The growth process takes you UP!

Where are you in the process of growth? Focus on this. It will bring long-term rewards. Also, know that the process of growth is a natural process. Enjoy it for what it brings to your dreams, efforts, and company!

The process of growth means that you will learn how to find talent, attract talent, make good hires, inspire performance, and create teamwork.

Culture in any organization starts at the top and can be amplified by those around you.

TEAM BUILDING: PART #4

—WHAT IT TAKES TO BE READY FOR THE BIG HIRE

As your business grows you will add people to your team. Along with tools and systems, they will give you leverage. They will allow you to serve more clients and get more done in less time. Having a great team of talented players ensures that your business will grow, persist, and prosper.

Each new hire will need to have specific skills, education, and knowledge that is appropriate to the role he will fulfill in your business. While you will provide on the job training and coaching, you want new hires to come with a readiness to handle the work. That is what you will look for and assess in your interviewing, hiring, and selection process.

But underneath these special abilities, you want all of your employees to be the SAME, which means:

> **S is for smart:** They are learning-based, trainable, and quick to understand.

> **A is for attractive:** They are well-groomed, neatly dressed, and pleasant to be with.

> **M is for motivated:** They are self-starters with a work ethic and ambition.

 > **E is for ethical:** They are honest, reliable, dependable, and trustworthy.

When you interview and when you check references, look for these traits. Seek some tangible evidence that they are there as you cannot train for them. They are already there or not. Be sure your people are, in this way, all the SAME!

You know what you want *IN* a person, but do you know what you want *OF* a person? That is the necessary next step.

Where the job hunt begins

The job hunt really takes shape when you create standards and operations manuals. This operating manual allows you to systemize and standardize processes in your business, which is precisely what you will require *OF* your employees.

Here are four important reasons to invest your time in creating a manual for your organization.

Create processes, expectations, and quality
- Provide consistent customer experiences – every time from every employee.
- Expectations should be clear and well-defined.
- Quality will be high for every transaction.

Better trained employees
- Document the tasks, processes, and quality; expectations can be used as training tools.
- Use this information so all employees are given the same information.
- Because of the documentation, others can train new employees.

Easier to expand your business
- If you open multiple locations, the standards and manuals create a plan that everyone must follow.
- Quality and processes are not left up to interpretation.

Make your business more valuable
- When you build a documented system for operating your business, you create value for your business. Prospective buyers will pay premium for a system that is documented, proven, and repeatable.

Here are some basic categories to include in your Operations Manual:

Contacts
- Vendors, partners, employees, maintenance/repairs, landlord

Task lists
- Create a list of tasks for each process in your business.
- Start with the daily routine-repeatable tasks.
- Create a detailed step-by-step process for each task: Use pictures, flow charts, diagrams.
- Have others use the process to refine and add detail.
- Organize by departmental function in the manual.

Troubleshooting
- This area answers the "what if" questions. Examples include:
    - Machine not working
    - Employee can't come to work
    - Injury in the work place

Guidelines/Policies
- Give employees guidelines on decision-making
- Customer guidelines are the first place to start (refunds, rescheduling, defective product)

The Operations Manual task lists

Your Operations Manual will include many task lists. You can add your own, but here are several to get the ball rolling:

Management Tasks
- One Page Strategic Plan (vision, mission, values, goals)
- Organizational Chart
- Team member position descriptions, contracts, goals, key performance indicators
- Recruitment System
- Orientation Program
- Leadership Development and Career Planning

Product Research and Development Tasks
- Develop products, intellectual property
- Develop packaging and collateral material such as catalogs, etc.
- Develop lean manufacturing methods and process
- Develop manufacturing costing and bidding process

Marketing, Lead Generation, and Sales Tasks
- Create and manage strategic marketing plan
- Create and manage sales management system
- Design and produce promotional materials
- Develop leads and prospects
- Create an advertising plan
- Create a public relations plan
- Create a direct mail plan

- Develop and maintain a database
- Develop and maintain a website
- Analyze and track sales data
- Continuously measure number and origin of all leads
- Measure conversion rate and average transaction value for each salesperson
- Measure average transaction value for every customer
- Measure profit margins for each product or service.

Order Processing and Tracking Tasks

- Take orders and record order by mail, fax, phone, or online
- Fulfill and package orders
- Confirm details before service or product delivery
- Send orders
- Create system for freight, couriers, and vehicles
- Maintain order tracking system

Manufacturing and Inventory Tasks

- Select vendors
- Maintenance of equipment
- Determine product or service warranties offered
- Establish product or service pricing
- Establish reorder process for inventory production
- Receive and store product as inventory
- Reconcile physical inventory with accounting records

Customer Service Tasks

- Return procedure for inventory receiving and customer payment return

  - Respond to customer complaints
  - Replace defective product or perform other warranty service

- Measure quality and professionalism of service delivery

Finance, Accounting, Legal Tasks
- Managing the accounting process with daily, weekly, monthly, quarterly, and annual reports
- Complete and manage monthly and yearly budgets and forecasts
- Complete weekly income statement
- Complete a monthly balance sheet
- Update daily or weekly cash flow statements
- Manage cash with future borrowing needs secured and available
- Report and deposit payroll tax and withholding payments
- Complete weekly bank reconciliation
- Daily banking activities
- Maintain an asset register including depreciation

Invoicing and Accounts Receivable Tasks
- Invoice customers for the orders
- Receive payments for orders and credit customer for payment
- Monitor credit control and age of accounts
- Start the collection process for outstanding receivables

Accounts Payable Tasks
- Payroll processing
- Purchasing procedures and approvals required
- Payment process for supplies and inventory
- Petty cash

Corporate Entity Tasks
- Negotiate, drafting, and executing contracts
- Develop and protect intellectual property

- Manage insurance needs and coverage
- Report and pay federal, state, and other taxes
- Planning for federal, state, and other taxes
- Manage and store records
- Maintain investor/shareholder relations
- Information flow processes
- Ensuring legal security
- Develop a business plan for planning and managing growth

Daily Office Physical Space Management Tasks
- Answer phones
- Receive and open mail
- Purchase and maintain office supplies and equipment
- Fax and email
- Dealing with incoming/outgoing delivery needs
- Backing up and archiving data
- Maintain and design telephone and electrical systems
- Upgrade office equipment
- Planning permits and fees
- Licensing
- Ensuring physical security

Behavioral questions

The talent search continues as you find out more about your prospects. The goal of asking behavioral questions is to find out if the person can do the job that you've so carefully outlined. It's important to recognize that past behavior can be a good indicator of future performance.

 The key phrases or words you use to create good questions will seek to tell you more about your prospect's past behavior. You'll be asking things like: Why? When? With whom? How long? How?

Here are a few good questions to keep in mind as you progress:

- Quick overview of your background and how it prepared you for this position.

- Can you give me a specific example?

- What did you do? What was the impact to the business? How did you do it?

- In this job you need to _____. How would you accomplish this? What relevant experience have you had?

> Your goal is to find out if the person can do the job that you have so carefully outlined.

- Share your favorite work experience.

- Share a time when your organization or team had a problem and how you helped solve the problem.

- Share a time when you took initiative to handle a difficult situation with a coworker.

- Draw out an organization chart for a project that you managed.

- Tell about a project you were totally committed to.

- What adjectives would you use to describe yourself? When have these traits helped you? When have they hindered you?

- Tell me about a take-home project you are working on.

Finding talent

People are the name of the game. As an entrepreneur, business owner, or business leader, the quality of your company will be determined by the quality of the people on your team. No matter how creative or powerful the vision, plan, and design, the venture will not flourish without talented people helping you. Be mindful of the company you keep. This starts with your team.

Getting great talent begins with knowing what and who you are looking for. The clarity that came from creating your operations manual has given you insight into the exact type of person you need to fill the specific role that you have.

Now, let's take things a step further.

TEAM BUILDING: PART #5

—NOW YOU ARE READY TO HIRE RIGHT

When you decide to add employees to your business, you want top talent. We've already discussed that this means they must be good at what they do, have a high work ethic, and be a dependable team player. They also need to want to learn, grow, and continually improve. And you must have your job description clearly defined as well.

The problem is how to find them because they are most likely already happily employed.

How do you find such people? The short answer is to use your network and send your need to them. The longer answer includes an explanation.

There is a three-step process to finding the right people. It is highly effective when you follow these steps.

Step #1: Missing Person's Report

The first step is to give your job prospects a description of what you need. Create what I call a "Missing Person Report" so you can share the specifics of what you are looking for in a new employee.

Include in the Missing Person Report such things as:

- Education: What education or certifications are necessary?
- Experience: What do they need to have done before?
- Skills: What do they need to do?
- Tasks: What specific duties will they need to perform?
- Attitude: What personality characteristics and behavioral styles do they need?

The Missing Person Report is a detailed description of the person you are looking for to fill that slot – the one who is currently missing from your business!

> Do you have a Missing Person Report for the job vacancy you have in your company ... right now?

If someone is going to help you find them and send them to you, they need to know what you're looking for. What are their skills? What education or experience is important? Do they have certain personality characteristics or behavioral styles that will make them successful in this work? What do they need to have done before?

Once you have this Missing Person Report done, you can send out an All-Points Bulletin to employment agencies, in the media, on Craigslist, to Master Networks members, and to your past clients. They will then increase the likelihood that the right person, the exact talent you seek, will come to you!

Recognize this:

> When they show up, you will recognize them, because they fit the description!

 The Missing Person Report matches the job description. That person is missing. You need them.

144

And then you can test the potential hire because you know what's needed. You are giving them a substantial accountability based description of what's needed. It's clear and in writing.

It requires that you, as you already have done, look closely at the business and understand what needs to be done, and done well, for the business to succeed. These are the tasks of your business, grouped into functions that form the precise job description.

> Your sphere of influence will gladly refer someone to you.

The job description that you have already created also helps you to better understand the skills, experience, attitudes, and behavior styles you are looking for in your hiring.

Step #2: Connect with the people you know

The second step is to connect with your contacts. They are your sphere of influence. And since they know you, trust you, and respect you, they are the perfect ones to tell about your Missing Person Report.

Most likely, they will know who would be a match for what you are looking for, even if that person is currently employed somewhere else.

Your message should include at least these three parts:

1) A sincere thank you
2) A description of who you are looking for
3) A request for their help

 The message begins with appreciation for their business, trust, and support. Next, talk about how business has grown and that you need a new world-class employee. Lastly, describe what that person looks like: education, experience, skills, attitudes, and aptitudes. Conclude with, "If you know someone who fits this description, let me know right away."

Your sphere of influence will gladly refer someone to you. Talent will always look at the right new opportunity. You just need to be introduced by someone they know. This is how it works.

Step #3: Set up a screening process

The third and final step is to set up a screening process to manage the candidates you receive. Use your Missing Person Report to create a scoring sheet that includes:

- Review for minimum qualifications – if they don't meet the minimum, do not score the other qualifications and do not interview.
- For those candidates meeting minimum qualifications, score them against the remaining qualifications you have set in the Missing Person Report. Interview the top scoring candidates.

The interview

For the interviews, you will need to be ready. I suggest that you focus on these areas:

Preparation
- Create interview questions based on the open job description.
- Review the candidate's application and resume right before the interview.

- Hold the interview in a location that is quiet and where you will not be interrupted.

Manage the Interview
- Opening: build rapport (welcome, thank you, excited to hear about your experiences related to the open position we have)
- Body: ask interviewee questions
- Close: interviewee asks you questions
- Conclusion: next steps

Note Taking
- Notes help you remember what the candidate shared versus your thoughts.
- Tell the interviewee you will be taking notes for future reference.
- Note highlights of their answers.
- Note behaviors you observe.
- Use key words and phrases.
- Fill in details after the interview.

References
- Ask for 3-4 references
- Majority should be industry related
- Have scripted, standard questions to ask everyone

Screening forms

As you screen out the candidates who are applying for the job you are listing, the following type of screening form may be of help:

Candidate Name: _____

 Reviewed by: _____

Date Reviewed: _____

Minimum Qualifications	Meets	Does Not Meet
BS in Management		
2 years in Leadership		
Interviewing		
Planning		

Perhaps you need to rate the candidates, comparing them to each other. This short preferred qualifications screening form may also be of value:

0: does not meet; 1: meets; 2: exceeds

	Rating	Notes
Experience		
Skills		
Tasks		

Sometimes the candidates will display traits or skills that make the process even easier. This may even help:

- ❑ Interview
- ❑ Do not Interview

Reference calls

If you do make reference calls, I would use something like this in your preparations:

Interviewee: _____

Reference: _____

Date called: ____

Hi, this is _____ (your name) with _____ (company name). _____ (Interviewee name) has applied for _____ (position title/short description) with my organization. You are listed as a reference; do you have time for a few questions?

In what capacity do you know the candidate?

How long have you known the candidate? How long did he/she work for you?

This position requires work in a team environment. Tell me about your experiences with _____ (candidate name) in a teamwork situation.

Those are all of my questions for today. Is there anything else you want to share with me to help in my decision making process?

By the way, who else should I talk to who could help me better understand this person and how might I work with him/her?

Adding to your team

After you choose to add the talented prospect to your company, it's time to graft him into the company that you hold so dear.

Joining your team is no small feat. This is a big deal! It's also a lot of fun.

TEAM BUILDING: PART #6

—CREATE THE CULTURE THAT YOU WANT & NEED

Once you find the right employees to join your organization, you want to welcome them with the knowledge and tools they need to be successful.

Rules of engagement

I suggest starting with your own Rules of Engagement that promote the culture you want for your organization.

These rules of engagement work best when they are written down and shared among all the people who are making a commitment to them. They become a standard for the business and the culture you enjoy together. You may even want to print them on posters and display them. They are often used to illustrate a point as stories about their use are shared.

Rules of engagement are a simple (not too wordy) list of the principles of conduct and communication that are valued and expected by everyone on the team. For example:

- Tell the truth
- Be accountable
- Show respect
- Give appreciation
- Do what you say you'll do

In order to be part of our team you have to sign a document that lays out the main components of our culture. We call the document "Commitment to Culture." It is not a contract but an agreement that we will abide by the culture we have created.

Short and sweet! The key is to make your own rules and get your team members involved in creating them. Then make it a document that everyone signs and commits to.

Great expectations

You will also want to set expectations, high expectations, for your people and processes. People tend to do what is expected of them and live up to the standards that are set.

You, as the leader, have to go first. You need to have high expectations for yourself. Also, others need to see you working as hard and taking on as much difficulty as anyone else on the team. Once you do this, you have earned the right to expect a lot from everyone else.

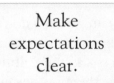

Make expectations clear.

You also need to make those expectations clear. When others know how you want the customers to be treated and how they should cooperate with one another, they share the success the team is aiming toward.

Finally, leaders must inspect what they expect. If the standard is being met, recognition, congratulations, and appreciation are delivered. If not, improvement and corrective action is asked for. Further investigation of the circumstances may reveal that training or coaching for the employee is needed to get him/her to meet expectations.

Helping employees who are not performing

Inevitably, some employees will fail to meet your expectations, fail to do a task properly, or fail in some other way. It is important that you find the real cause. To determine the underlying cause, start by asking the employee to explain and/or demonstrate a job task while you simply observe. You should be able to easily determine what went wrong. Perhaps it was:

Knowledge or Skills

If they simply don't know how to perform the task, then they have not yet developed the proper skills. Follow up with re-training or coaching.

Process

If the issue is caused by working conditions, bad processes, etc., then the employee isn't at fault. Work with the employee(s) to remove the obstacles they are facing.

Resources

If the issue is a lack of resources or technology impeding them, again work to remove the challenges and ensure they have the appropriate resources to succeed.

Motivation or Culture

If the employee knows what to do and has the proper resources and process but does not perform to expectations, then further conversations are necessary. Perhaps the person is not motivated, doesn't enjoy the work, or it simply is not the correct job for him/her. Also explore the issue of culture and rewards. Are the rewards supporting the expectations and goals set? Is the team holding the person back because working too hard makes everyone else look bad?

Are you a boss or a coach?

When you determine an employee needs coaching, keep in mind a coach has a different set of expectations from a boss. Consider this reality:

Things a Boss may do	Things a Coach may do
• Pushes and drives	• Lifts and supports
• Tells/directs/lectures	• Asks/requests/listens
• Talks at people	• Engages in dialogue with people
• Controls through decisions	• Facilitates by empowering
• Knows the answer	• Seeks the answer
• Triggers insecurity using fear to achieve	• Stimulates creativity using purpose to inspire
• Points to errors	• Celebrates learning
• Problem solver/decision maker	• Collaborator/facilitator
• Delegates responsibility	• Models accountability
• Creates structure and procedures	• Creates vision and flexibility
• Does things right	• Does the right things
• Knowledge is power	• Vulnerability is power
• Focused on the bottom line	• Focused on process to create bottom-line results

No doubt you want to be a coach rather than a dictator boss! Here are several examples of what a coach will do:

- Provide employees with information, instructions, and suggestions relating to their job assignments and performance.

- Be a cheerleader and facilitator to guide employees' behaviors toward the desired results.

- Create a healthy, positive, and enabling process to develop the capacity of employees to solve today's business problems.
- Help people identify and connect to their role in the organization.
- Guide and challenge people to meet their goals.
- Tutor employees so they gain knowledge, competency, and skill.
- Counsel employees – noticing problems and helping gain insight into and assist in solving them.

3C's to coaching

As a reminder of what it means to be a coach:

1. **Connection**
   - Build rapport.
   - Help employees understand importance of their performance to the organization.
   - Create a positive, trusting environment.

2. **Conversation**
   - Share and explain the expectations and goals of coaching.
   - Ask for employees' perspective and listen.
   - Have an ongoing dialogue at scheduled intervals.

3. **Commitment**
   - Create an agreement of expectations and timeline.
   - Discuss resources needed.

TEAM BUILDING: PART #8

—WORKING SMOOTHLY TOGETHER AS A TEAM

One of the biggest challenges for a business owner or leader is creating teamwork, cooperation, and collaboration. It is the fabric of a company that is effectively working in harmony.

Thousands of books have been written and seminars delivered trying to teach leaders how to build effective, high-performance teams. But for the wisest, most mature entrepreneurs, it's not that complicated to build teamwork, motivation, and morale.

What's the secret? There isn't just one secret, as there are many parts of the puzzle, but one very big element is this: connection.

The power of connection

Great leaders help their people feel good about what they do, the people they do it with, and the customers they serve. These leaders help everyone understand the mission, values, vision, and goals of the business. They help each one understand the important role he or she plays in making the team successful in its accomplishing and fulfilling of the company goals and mission.

Research about what is important to employees revealed a curious conflict in point of view. When asked, "What do employees most want?" business owners listed: good wages, job security, and promotion opportunities.

What did the employees actually say they valued? Interestingly, their top three needs were: appreciation for their work, feeling "in" on things, and sympathetic help on personal problems.

The issue of building a great team is simply helping people feel connected. That means you tell them you appreciate what they do, include them in on important business information, discussions, and planning, and create an environment where all the people care about each other personally.

> Build the right business culture and productive teamwork will thrive!

Build this business culture and productive teamwork will thrive!

Leaders are always concerned with getting the team to perform at a high level. Businesses thrive when the owner and leaders know how to motivate great work.

Of course, it begins with attracting and hiring people who already have positive attitudes and good work habits. Motivation is, above all, an inside job. But leaders get the best out of the talent they have and they maximize performance.

Culture of feedback needed

As you expand your business, add more people, and take on more complex operations, it will be a challenge to stay entrepreneurial, energized, and light on your feet.

As the leader, you will need an accurate picture of what is happening, how your people are performing, and what needs to be changed. For a multi-layered, multiple-department business, this is not easy.

The typical chain-of-command organization that allows us to divide labor and maintain control can also get in the way of creativity, communication, and progress. The business can get stuck in its own protocols and operating regulations. It can become bureaucratic and stodgy.

The cure for this is setting up "skip level" or "bypass the chain" communication mechanisms. Allow for anonymous suggestion boxes for feedback messages. Hold skip level confidential meetings with employees. Encourage all your departmental leaders to pass along ideas, suggestions, and criticisms.

Have 360-degree performance evaluations where all team members are allowed to confidentially rate the work and contribution of everyone on the team, including the supervisors. Use these feedback systems to help you in coaching people toward better performance and more effective leadership.

Knowing that they can speak up empowers everybody and makes them feel they are a part of the team. And the feedback creates true accountability for all. In the end, it will keep your business alert, energized, and creative as it grows.

Culture of communication

One of the biggest keys to working smoothly, within the company and with everyone who relates to the company, is to have an open line of communication. This comes as no surprise to any of us, for great communication is the lubricant of all effective relationships.

 For those who are intentional about what we are doing and the results we intend, communication cannot be neglected or simply hoped for. You must be open and clear about how you will communicate with each other. For the team to accomplish great things they must know where they stand.

How to handle meetings

Every team needs to have meetings, just like a football team has a huddle or a basketball team reviews game film or a charity project holds a planning session. As our businesses grow, there will be an ever-increasing need to meet with our people, gather them together, and coordinate their work.

The problem is that most people don't like the meetings they are asked to attend. What's more, most meetings are a pure waste of time, and thus money!

As the business leader, you need to get good at holding effective, interesting, high-performance meetings! This is a vital skill to build. Here is a short overview of the most basic elements of a successful meeting:

- start on time
- end on time
- keep it short
- follow the agenda
- keep them moving

One of the lessons I have learned over time that helps to set the right tone in our meetings is to start with something we refer to as bucket filling. We start by expressing gratitude for other team members' work over the past two weeks. For example, "Ed, thank you for your work on the XYZ project! You were fantastic and so helpful!"

We find that it starts the meeting off on the right foot. Additionally, we also use this time to be accountable for past assignments. It is quite something to show up and have to report to the entire team my progress on assignments.

This time with your team should be one of accountability and sharing of ideas. One mistake I often observe is leaders giving their opinion and then asking for others to give their input. Then they wonder why nobody else has a comment. Give your team the opportunity to give input and feedback before you share your thoughts. You will find out that they have much to contribute. Many times they have a better idea or plan than I had before.

> Give your team the opportunity to give input and feedback *before* you share your thoughts.

I recommend that you hold your meetings at the same time every week and build the expectation that everyone should be there and ready to go before the start time.

Shorten the time allotted for the meeting. In many cases, it is best to make them stand-up meetings of less than 15 minutes.

Following an agenda really means that you know the purpose of the meeting and what needs to be accomplished during that time. Stephen Covey says, "Begin with the end in mind." That really applies to meetings. What must we get done before we leave? What specific information do we need to share and what decisions do we need to make? Let everyone know what the agenda is.

Once this is in place, your job as leader is to keep the session focused, dynamic, and on-track. Everyone on the team will positively look forward to meeting because they are good and effective – as they should be!

Score cards

There are times when you need to evaluate people on your team, whether for a raise or some other reason. This score card system may help:

Name: _____

Position: _____

Hire Date: _____

Today's Date: _____

Prepared by: _____

Grading System:

4 pts = Often exceeds expectations

    15-20 pts = ____ % raise in hourly pay

3 pts = Consistently meets expectations

    10-15 pts = ____ % raise in hourly pay

2 pts = Sometimes meets expectations

    5-10 pts = ____ % raise in hourly pay

1 pt = Below expectations

    0-5 pts = no raise (needs improvement)

0 pts = Unacceptable

Job Function	Manager's Comments	Points	Employee's Comments
Customer Service Skills • hospitality • telephone manners • exceed customer expectations • professional appearance and demeanor			
Financial Skills • understand quotes • answer basic questions • follow up with customers on payment • make purchasing decisions with budget in mind			
System Skills • compliance manual • cluster booking • timeliness on completing tasks			
Services • explain services offered • articulate quality standards			
Teamwork • demonstrate positive attitude • assist coworkers • professionalism • maintain composure under stress or busy times • treat everyone with respect			
Overall Rating			

Signatures: _____ (manager)

_____ (employee)

Understanding behavior

As you continually work to create a culture that helps your business grow and succeed, there may be times when you need to dig a little deeper into the behavior of your employees.

Nobody has done anything wrong! But the more you understand about the people you work with, the more you are going to say, "Oh, now I know why he does that" or "Now I understand why she thinks that."

> The more you understand and appreciate each other, the more cohesion you have as a team.

The more you understand and appreciate each other, the more cohesion you have as a team, and that only helps propel you faster toward success!

With people in general, some people just seem to "get you" and working with them is easy and almost effortless. Others just view the world so differently and working together on projects is harder to the point of frustration.

Using a tool, such as DiSC, can help you understand your own behaviors. Once you are grounded in your own preferences and styles, you can use DiSC to understand others and work together more effectively. You will even start appreciating the differences others bring! I've seen it happen.

Here is an overview of the four DiSC styles. Though the terms themselves will be helpful, taking the test yourself will give you even more clarity:

Dominance
- Direct
- Results-oriented
- Firm

- Strong-willed
- Forceful

Influence
- Outgoing
- Enthusiastic
- Optimistic
- High-spirited
- Lively

Steadiness
- Even-tempered
- Accommodating
- Patient
- Humble
- Tactful

Conscientiousness
- Analytical
- Reserved
- Precise
- Private
- Systematic

The DiSC profile can be helpful as you hire new employees, put teams together for special projects, and coach employees. Understanding yourself and your employees will bring about great synergy and productivity for you organization.

 In business, "smooth" translates into more business, efficiency, effectiveness, and at the bottom line more money.

Learning to work with and coach all different behavioral styles is the mark of a great leader. The key is helping others understand how they can get the most out of themselves and to work with others.

As leaders, we must do more to build and develop others and do less to draw attention to ourselves.

Team Building Summary

- Successful entrepreneurs know that they will not do anything significant alone.
- Your goal is to have less to do, not more!
- Building a team doesn't need to be complicated.
- The path to Leverage: I do it. We do it. They do it!

CHAPTER SIX

The Master Skill

"The master skill is both the glue that holds all the pieces together and oil that makes it all operate smoothly."
—Dave Jenks

PART #1

—THE MASTER SKILL

I have often heard the phrase, "It's not what you know, but rather who you know that counts." Even more important than those who you know are those who know you!

This point was further validated to me when I started to read and study some classic business books. One of my early reads was *Rich Dad Poor Dad* by Robert Kiyosaki.

Kiyosaki taught that to be a successful business owner I needed to invest in a team. His team was comprised of his accountant, attorney, brokers, insurance agent, business banker, and financial advisor. He learned that working with his team was the best education he could gain because building the business with his team helped him learn more than he ever could on his own.

Kiyosaki is proof to one of the truest success principles I know:

Successful business owners don't do it alone!

As a new business owner, I learned quickly that if I wanted to be more successful, I needed to build relationships with more people.

Networking Marketing

If you ask any business owner what the most powerful form of marketing or advertising is that brings them the greatest return on their money and brings the best kind of customer, they unanimously say, "Word-of-mouth."

Why?

First, it is powerful in its nature because people have gone out of their way to endorse you and encourage that contact to use your business to meet their needs.

> Successful business owners don't do it alone.

Second, you typically are spending any revenue directly to acquire that business. Lastly, more often than not, if I am going to refer someone to you I have probably used your service. This means I already know what kind of customer would be best for you and I am almost pre-qualifying the referral for you. This makes your job of "selling" so much easier once you receive the referral.

The Lost Skill of Networking

Technology has never been more accessible. I can send a message to someone halfway across the world in an instant. We can communicate electronically in seconds. In fact, email, instant chat or messaging, and social media have even developed their own sort of language. Emoticons, Hashtags, and other forms of communication have developed as a way to further share the message.

Recently I went to a large training conference. During the conference I visited the large exhibitor hall where many vendors had booths set up looking to showcase and demonstrate their products. I was amazed as I walked up and down each row looking at each and every booth, I noticed that almost nobody looked up from their phones to engage me in discussion.

I thought to myself, "Why even have someone at the booth if they won't take two seconds to look up from their phone to tell me about their product."

Imagine the difference if they stood up, looked me in the eye, asked me my name, and shook my hand as they introduced themselves.

I recently helped my son work on a Science Fair project. He was really proud of what he had put together. His project was great! As we drove to the location of the science fair, I asked if we could practice what he was going to do and say when the judges came to his booth.

I shared that the project was only half of the presentation and he needed to be able to communicate the project as well. "When the judges come to your booth I want you to stand up and say, 'Hi, my name is Ryan. I am a sixth-grader, and I would like to share with you why I decided to do this project.'"

We practiced several times on the way. When the time came and the judges approached his booth, I watched as he delivered just how we practiced. I was amazed at how he was the only one to stand and look the judges in the eye. He had each judge completely captivated in his presentation.

He was thrilled when he viewed the results and had nearly a perfect score in every category. More importantly, I saw a young man have confidence when he was able to communicate his message.

 Networking starts with an ability to communicate and build on your common interests. Networking is a skill that can be learned. And, if it can be learned, it can be taught!

The Method

There was a time when networking for me meant going to business socials where other entrepreneurs gathered for appetizers and small talk. This was neither fun nor effective.

Then, I was introduced to some more formal concepts of networking. This was an improvement, but I felt these methods were shallow and lacked the depth of building true relationships.

> Networking is a skill, a skill that can be learned!

Truly effective networking is focused on the building of long-lasting, trusted relationships. Those take time to build.

A few years ago, I was asked to lunch by a young man who worked at a local bank. As a new business banker he was instructed to go network. With no real clear understanding of what that meant and how to effectively build relationships, he was left to make it up.

He asked me if I would join him for lunch so that he could learn more about my business, Master Networks, and how he might be able to help me.

We met at the arranged location and sat down. We ordered our food and made quick introductions. For the next 45 minutes I didn't say a word. I heard about his love of cars, how he traded stocks, and how the bank was a short term job in his climb to being an entrepreneur.

As we finished our food and I got up to leave, he said, "We should do this again soon." Rather surprised and mostly because I wanted to leave, I replied, "Sure."

As I left, I realized that this disaster of a lunch wasn't really his fault. He hadn't been trained or taught how to effectively build relationships. How to find out and discover who I am and what I need. Without that, how could he ever help me?

I went directly back to my office and gathered my team to dissect and discuss every step of how we have effectively built a national organization completely on relationships we had developed over time.

What we had mastered was the B.O.N.D Method!

This B.O.N.D. method will give you the model to follow and empower you to create efficient and effective meetings with clients and potential customers. It is also an effective way to maximize your scheduled meetings, chance encounters, and large networking events.

When you have practiced and mastered the B.O.N.D. method, you will discover partnerships, create focus for meetings, build mutually beneficial relationships, and grow your business!

PART #2

—B is for BUILDING ON COMMON INTERESTS

Start with the foundation. When building a new home, if you do not have a solid foundation, the rest of the home will fall apart.

This first step takes time. It is the most important. If you rush this step, you may not ever get the chance to move forward.

The most important concept to remember here is that you are trying to make a connection. Connection is key!

B: Build on common interests

- Find a common interest to build a connection
- Show interest
- Ask what they have done
- Discover how they ended up at your chance meeting

Put it into Practice

The key to using B.O.N.D. lies in your ability to manage the meeting and move from a casual conversation to a potential strategic partnership. Building on a common interest creates rapport and a connection. Finding that connection is key to building the foundation necessary to move forward. Without a connection, the person may be reluctant to move the conversation in a productive direction.

Here are some tips to keep in mind as you build on a common interest:

- Be curious and ask good questions. Do not make this a competition or make it about you!
- Don't overuse the "I'm like you" connection.
- Be genuine and caring in your conversation.
- Have questions ready and prepared.
- Make them feel important and do it sincerely.
- Smile!

Asking good questions and then actively listening are two ways to show interest. The quality of the answers you will get are directly related to the quality of the questions you ask. Use follow-up and probing questions to get the information you need.

Here are some sample questions you can use to build on a common interest:

- How do you spend your free time?
- How far did you drive?
- What brings you to this event?
- Do you have a favorite vacation destination?
- Are you enjoying the conference? What do you like best so far?
- What have you learned from this training/conference/event?
- Do you have pets? Kids?
- Are you from this area originally?
- What hobbies do you have? What makes that fun for you?

- Favorite book/movie/TV show/song?
- What would your perfect day look like?
- What time of day/year do you like best?
- Best life lesson learned from coach/parent/aunt/ grandparent?
- Favorite childhood game/memory/hobby.
- What famous person would you spend time with?
- What magazines or books do you read?
- Look for visual cues: lapel pin, hat, shirt, car, etc. and ask them about it.

Mastering the B.O.N.D. method can bring about the collaborative partnerships necessary to build your business, focus your time during any type of face-to-face meeting, build mutually beneficial relationships, and grow your business.

B.O.N.D.: PART #3

—O is for OCCUPATION EXPLORATION

The Occupation Exploration step of B.O.N.D. is focused on their work. Your goal is to continue building connections with people and learn more about their career, which leads to greater insight into who they are. The more you know about what they do and how they got there, the easier you will discover needs and develop opportunities.

Occupation Exploration

Good questions get you more in-depth answers to discover:

- Their passion and understanding of their "why."
- The path they've taken and how one thing leads to another.
- Steps in their journey, which gives insight into their values and ideals.

During this phase of B.O.N.D., keep these tips in mind:

- Keep the conversation about them – limit your air time.
- Have a goal in mind when you ask questions.
- Be prepared if the conversation gets off track – bring it back around to relevant information.
- Some of the questions may not be appropriate for a first meeting.
- Be open to the many careers people choose (stay at home parents, corporate, blue collar). They all have needs.

Here are some questions that work well for the Occupation phase of B.O.N.D.:

- How did you get interested in your line of work?
- Have you always been in this industry? If no, what made you change?
- What do you like most about what you do?
- What changes have you seen in your industry in the last year?
- What is your biggest accomplishment in your career?
- What about your job/industry keeps you up at night?
- How do you obtain new customers? How successful is that method?
- What one sentence would you want people to use when describing the way you do business?
- If you could be wherever you want and do whatever you want, what would it be?
- Which of your competitors do you admire most?
- What separates you from your competitors?
- What is your organization's greatest strength?
- What does your ideal customer look like?
- What does your career look like 5-10 years out?
- What business related books have you read lately?

> **Keep thinking as you progress.**

As the conversation progresses, start thinking about and asking questions to uncover the business needs this person may have. For example, if a stay-at-home parent just returned to work, he/she may need a house cleaning service. A chiropractor, for example, could ask how someone normally handles the frequent headaches they have.

Keep thinking as you progress, but don't jump ahead. That is a vital part of the process as you build rapport and trust.

B.O.N.D.: PART #4

—N is for NEEDS DISCOVERY

The time you spend Building on Common Interests and Occupation Exploration builds the element of rapport. Be sure you have spent enough time and have established a foundation of trust before moving to Needs Discovery.

If you rush the conversation, they may not feel you are coming from a spirit of contribution. Be clear that your intention is one of "How can I help?" versus "What can I sell you?"

By spending time in this process, they will understand that you truly want to help them.

Needs Discovery

Needs Discovery is an important bridge from the B and O steps to Develop Opportunity, so take the time to prepare. Write down scripts and practice what you want to say during this step. Jot down questions you may want to use and have them ready if you have a lull in the conversation.

Here are some questions you may want to use:

- What are you trying to accomplish?
- What results have you achieved so far?
- Where are you stuck?
- What kinds of problems are you encountering?
    - What are your goals?
    - What frustrates you about that situation?

- What solutions have you tried?
- Is this issue something you have time and energy to work on?
- What would happen if you did resolve this issue?
- What has gotten more challenging for you since that change?
- What is the greatest challenge you will face in the next year?
- What is the biggest threat to your business?
- What right now would make the most positive impact on your business?

Think about what the person said during the first part of your conversation and pick out those things they seem to be frustrated or dissatisfied with. Focus on those things and ask pointed questions to discover how you might help.

This is when you can be bold and share the story of your business. Share what you do and how you have helped others and express your passion to help them.

B.O.N.D.: PART #5

—D is for DEVELOPING OPPORTUNITIES

The B.O.N.D. model is funnel-shaped, but as you well know, not every conversation will move through all the steps to an opportunity. Some conversations end after Build on Common Interest or Occupation Exploration because of time constraints or circumstance or lack of interest. You may even get to the Needs Discovery stage and at that point realize there is not an opportunity.

This is where continued practice on this skill becomes valuable. Your ability to discover the needs and now move to developing opportunities that are mutually beneficial is where the real skill in networking is.

Success in Developing Opportunities requires:

- Recognizing good opportunities early
- Moving from pulling information to sharing of information
- Focusing on finding solutions to fix problems

Here are examples of different opportunities to explore:

- Sale of product and/or service
- New Master Network's member
- Referral for you or someone in your chapter
- Co-branding (people who need your services/products need mine)
  - Joint event (chiropractor – fitness – financial planner offered educational seminar)

- Co-marketing
- Partnerships (three chiropractors in one chapter, each with a different specialty)
- Sponsor Events – trade product/services for sponsorship

Phrases or questions to ask as you Develop an Opportunity

- Knowing what I do, how can I help you?
- What if there is a solution?
- How do you see us working together?
- What if . . . (getting their introspection)
- Other people in your situation have benefitted from . . .
- A few minutes ago you mentioned . . . (use their words)
- What solutions have you attempted?
- What do you see as your options?
- Do you want input from me?
- What is our "go forward" plan?
- Have you ever thought of trying "x." I am using "x" and here are the results I am having.
- When could you meet to discuss further?

Many of us enjoy small talk and catching up on life when we meet. However, you want to ensure your conversations move on to the Develop Opportunity step of the B.O.N.D. method.

Don't limit yourself to offering your products or services to the other person. Take time to explore the chance of creating strategic partnerships, which come in many different forms.

Here are some examples:

- **Sales** of products or services
- **Co-Marketing**: appropriate when clients of your services are likely to need services of another chapter member in your sphere. Examples: real estate agent and handy man sharing links on websites

(chiropractor focused on kids and a music academy)

- **Co-Branding**: consider this tactic when your services are integral to another service. Example: chiropractic and massage
- **Open House Events**: several chapter members from a sphere can host an open house, as their customer bases have similar wants/needs. Example: environmental friendly cleaning, healthy supplements, Chiropractic, jewelry
- **Shared Office Space**: useful when clients have dependent needs. Example: massage therapy, fitness center, and nutrition counseling.
- **Special Offers for Clients**: create special rates or offers for clients of others within your sphere. Example: A house cleaning service can offer reduced rates on move-in cleaning for the clients of the real estate agent in his/her chapter.
- **Joint Booths at Conferences/Expos**: expos can offer a wide reach to many potential customers; however, the costs can be prohibitive. Partner with someone in your sphere to share costs and labor.

Be strategic about the partnerships you build. Note that many of the examples focused on finding other members who have clients with similar or dependent needs. Focusing on collaboration ensures that both parties will benefit from the partnership.

The more you B.O.N.D., the more you will realize there are strategic partnerships everywhere!

One of the best opportunities for the person you are meeting with may be with someone else. Imagine the B.O.N.D. you would build with this person if you saw a need and knew of someone else who could help. Coming from contribution is the only way this works!

Stay ON

When I'm out and about, I am on. I'm looking for cues and ways to B.O.N.D. Sometimes I'll offer info or advice, but I'm thinking, "How in general can I help this person?"

Of course you have to be genuine and not distracted, but recognize that not every conversation is going to go right through the funnel. And some people will bail out part of the way through. That's okay!

Be mindful of their time, so be as efficient as you can. Annoying isn't an option.

> Your ability to discover the needs and now move to developing opportunities that are mutually beneficial is where the real skill in networking is!

Remember, you are building mutually beneficial relationships as you grow your business. When that is the goal, you can't go wrong!

B.O.N.D. Summary

- Networking is the master skill!
- Successful entrepreneurs build their network!
- Relationships are key! The human connection will not be replaced.

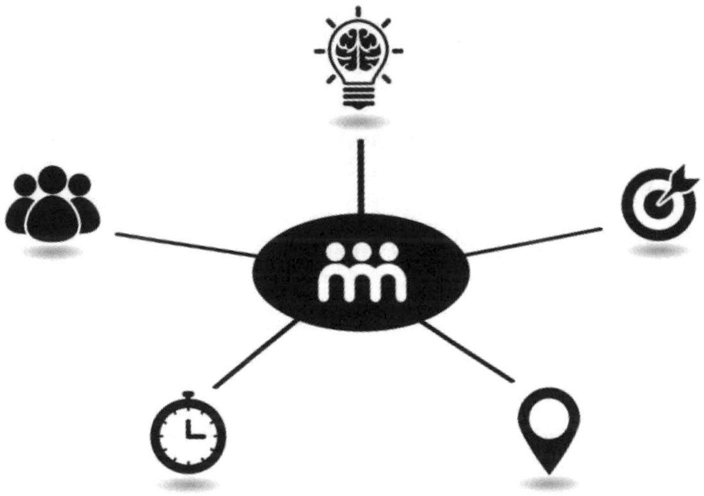

CONCLUSION

What is today's date? Look at your watch, phone, or calendar. Remember it well, for it is the date that will forever be remembered as the day you became accountable for all you have learned!

That's good news because we are talking about real, practical growth! The principles you have learned, held together and oiled with the B.O.N.D. system, are ready to be applied to your life and business today.

You have the steps. They are like a train track, a clear pathway that you can implement and follow. They will take you wherever you are going!

Armed with these skills, you are on task, on target, and on fire! Your competition had better watch out!

Find a local Master Network group to join to keep the intensity and accountability going. If there isn't a group in your area, then start one.

You are on our team, and we are on yours, so don't hesitate to reach out if there is something we can do to help you grow and succeed. That's what we do ... together.

For further resources and downloads please visit:

www.FiveplusOneBook.com

MASTER NETWORKS

We are a membership network of learning-based, service-oriented entrepreneurs and business leaders. We meet in local chapters, powered by national and regional platforms, to connect, share, and prosper.

On a weekly basis, members have a full hour to focus on themselves and their businesses. They have the opportunity to teach others about their business via one minute sound bites and ten minute show case presentations. The business training and personal development topics presented each week push them to work *on* their business, not just *in* their business. The referrals received from fellow chapter members help their business grow and their return on investment is realized.

Members can also step into leadership positions to have a direct impact on the excitement, growth, and energy of their chapters. Contribution and involvement of members leads to an even greater sense of connection to their Master Networks Chapters.

To learn more about Master Networks or to find a chapter near you, visit:

www.MasterNetworks.com

NEXT LEVEL SUITE

We have made arrangements for our readers to get a special discount by entering the promo code "book" during checkout.

Next Level Suite is a simple to use and cost effective solution for a business to manage contacts. I use this system daily to communicate with my clients and prospects.

NEXT LEVEL COACHING

Next Level Coaching is the delivery method in which we help business leaders and entrepreneurs implement the steps learned in the pages on this book.

I travel the country teaching and training the Five Plus One formula and I am always being asked, "What now?" "How do I make this happen?" Next Level Coaching is the solution and answer to that question.

Visit my site to request a complementary coaching call at:
www.ChasWilson.com

ACKNOWLEDGMENTS

I want to thank my wife Jaclyn and our five children: Ryan, McKenzie, Breydan, Jack, and Tate. You have all taught me so much and you are my inspiration. Jaclyn, you are such an amazing support, partner, and friend. Thank you for encouraging me along the way. I love you!

Thank you to my parents, Kent and Lynn, for your love, always believing in me, and supporting me.

Terry and Jody for your faith in me and for your support.

Ed LeQuire, you are an amazing business partner and friend! I appreciate your loyalty and support.

I want to thank my friend and colleague Dave Jenks for his work with Master Networks University and as a brainstorming partner.

Katelyn and Sara, thank you for all you do each day to support my vision. I couldn't do it without you!

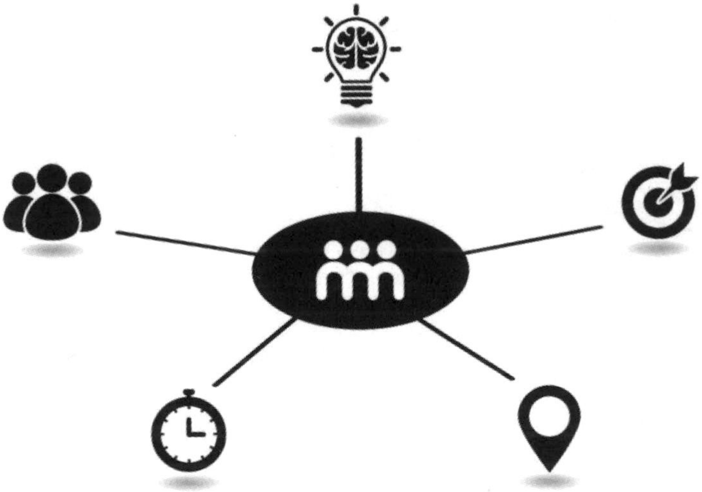